ThickSkin

IT WALKS AROUND THE HOUSE AT NIGHT

by Tim Foley

It Walks Around The House At Night was first performed at Chichester Festival Theatre on Wednesday 4 February 2026.

Cast

Joe	George Naylor
The Dancer	Oliver Baines

Featuring the voice of Paul Hilton

Creative Team

Writer	Tim Foley
Director	Neil Bettles
Sound Design	Pete Malkin
Lighting & Video Design	Joshua Pharo
Set Design	Neil Bettles & Tom Robbins
Design Associate (Costume)	Madison Omatseone
Associate Director	Anna Berentzen
Sound Associate	Kieran Lucas
Dramaturg	Brendan Macdonald
Casting Director	Claire Bleasdale

Production Team

Production Managers	Tom Robbins
	Brent Tan
Company Stage Manager	Madeleine Coward
Technical Stage Manager	Emily Foster
Relighter	Grace Bastyan

For ThickSkin

Artistic Director	Neil Bettles
Executive Producer	Laura Mallows
Senior Producer	Steph Connell
Associate Producer	Abi Beaven
Assistant Producer	Rae Bell
Head of Marketing & Audiences	Iain Christie
Marketing Agency	Make A Noise
Press & PR Management	Chloe Nelkin Consulting

A ThickSkin Production. Supported by Arts Council England.

With thanks to: Dominic Coffey, Hannah Clapham-Clark, Louise Fazackerley, Neil Harris, Joshua Hill, Susan Jones, Lamin Touray, James Westphal, Jerome Yates, Hawkseed Theatre, White Light.

Cast

George Naylor | Joe

George (he/him) is an actor who trained at the Royal Welsh College of Music and Drama. Theatre credits include: *Second Best*, (Riverside Studios); *Room 13* (Barn Theatre, Cirencester); *The Mousetrap* (West End, UK Tour); *Wendy & Peter* (The Royal Lyceum Edinburgh); *One Man Two Guv'nors* (Torch Theatre); *Much Ado About Nothing* (Heartbreak Theatre). Screen credits include: *Casualty* (BBC); *Open* (Restless Native's); *Muttersprache, Sundowning* and *Hangnail* (NFTS); *Re-Live* (BFI); and *King Arthur: Excalibur Rising* (Tornado Films). As voiceover: *Cicero*, *The Box of Delights* and multiple *Doctor Who* and *Torchwood* episodes (Big Finish Productions); *The Sandman* series III, *Scarlet City* and *The Waringham Chronicles* (Audible). Video game credits: *Final Fantasy* (Square Enix); *Baldur's Gate III* (Larian Studios); *Metaphor Refantazio* (Sega); *Dragon Quest III* (Chunsoft); *Sea of Remnants* (NetEase); and *Transformers: Shadow Rising* (Sega). He was a Carleton Hobbs Finalist, an Alan Bates Award Runner Up, and recipient of the John Gielgud Award.

Oliver Baines | The Dancer

Oliver Baines (he/him) is an actor, musician, and dancer from Manchester. Oliver trained through the Frantic Assembly Ignition Programme. For ThickSkin he performed in short films *The City* and *Ancoats*. Theatre credits include: *The House Party* (Headlong/Frantic Assembly/Chichester Festival Theatre, UK Tour); *Lost & Found* (Factory International); *Othello* (Frantic Assembly, UK Tour); *SoftLad* (WonderIfTheatre).

Creative Team

Tim Foley | Writer

Tim Foley (he/him) is an award-winning writer for theatre and audio drama based in Manchester. Work for ThickSkin: *Driftwood* (with Pentabus, UK Tour). Previous theatre work includes *Jurassic* (Ransack Theatre); *Electric Rosary* (Royal Exchange Theatre); *Astronauts of Hartlepool* (VAULT Festival); *The Dogs of War* (Old Red Lion Theatre). Audio drama credits: *Murder On Mars* (BBC Radio 4); *Doctor Who* (Big Finish Productions); *North West Footwear Database* (BBC Radio 4 Extra). Awards include the Bruntwood Prize Judges' Award, the VAULT Origins Award for outstanding new work, OffWestEnd's Most Promising New Playwright.

Neil Bettles | Director & Set Design

Neil (he/him) is a director, choreographer and movement director. As co-founder and

Artistic Director of ThickSkin his directing credits include: *Pigeon, Driftwood, Only The Beginning, Peak Stuff, How Not To Drown, Shade, Chalk Farm, Boy Magnet, Bring Your Own, The Static* and *Blackout*, and for ThickSkin's Walk This Play series: *Keep Going Then Vanish, Your Time Now* and *This Is Where We Begin*. Other directing credits: *The Unreturning, This Will All Be Gone* and *No Way Back* (Frantic Assembly). As Choreographer: *Assassins* (Chichester Festival Theatre); *Bedknobs and Broomsticks* (Disney, UK and Ireland tour). As Movement Director: *Make Good* (Pentabus); *Great Expectations* (Royal Exchange Theatre); *James IV, Queen Of The Fight,* (Raw Material and Capital Theatres, Scottish tour); *Private Peaceful* (Jonathan Church Theatre Productions & Nottingham Playhouse); *Carmen* (Opera Wuppertal, Germany); *The James Plays I, II and III* (National Theatre of Scotland, Edinburgh International Festival and National Theatre); *Blood Wedding and The Bacchae* (Royal & Derngate). As Associate Movement Director: *Harry Potter and the Cursed Child* (Sonia Friedman Productions, worldwide); *Heisenberg* (Wyndhams Theatre); *The Light Princess* (National Theatre) and *The Full Monty* (Sheffield Theatres & West End). As Associate Director: *Disco Show* (La Mama, New York). Neil has received multiple awards for his work at ThickSkin.

Pete Malkin | Sound Design

Pete Malkin (he/him) is a sound designer that trained at the Royal Central School of Speech and Drama. Sound Design credits include: *Brighter Still* (Bradford City of Culture Closing Ceremony); *Otherland* (Almeida Theatre); *Robin/Red/Breast* (Factory International); *Midsummer Night's Dream* (RSC); *Let the Right One In, Death of a Salesman, Queens of the Coal Age* (Royal Exchange); *There is a Light That Never Goes Out: Scenes from the Luddite Rebellion* (Royal Exchange/Kandinsky); *The Cherry Orchard* (Simon McBurney, Toneelgroep Amsterdam); *Privacy* (Kilden Theatre Norway); *The Unreturning* (Frantic Assembly); *Pity* (Royal Court); *Schism* (Park Theatre); *The Kid Stays in the Picture* (Complicité/Royal Court); *The Tempest* (Donmar Warehouse/St Ann's Warehouse); *Beware of Pity* (Complicité); *Frogman* (Curious Directive); *Treasure, Home Chat* (Finborough); *Unearthed* (Folio Theatre); *Am I Dead Yet* (Unlimited Theatre); *War Correspondents* (Helen Chadwick/Steven Hoggett, UK Tour); *The Commission/Café Kafka* (Aldeburgh, Linbury Studio, Opera North); *SUN* (National Art Service); *Farragut North* (Southwark Playhouse); *Space Junk* (Lyric/Gameshow); *Marguerite* (Tabard Theatre). As Co-Sound Designer: *Othello* (National Theatre); *The Chairs* (Almeida Theatre) *Death of*

England: The Trilogy (National Theatre); The Encounter (Complicité); The Noise (Unlimited Theatre). As Associate Sound Designer: Harry Potter and the Cursed Child (West End); 1984 (Headlong); The Magic Flute (ENO/Complicité); Lionboy (Complicité); Hamlet (RSC); Rock Pool (Inspector Sands); Die Zauberflöte (Simon McBurney, DNO/Complicite). Pete won multiple awards for Complicité and Simon McBurney's The Encounter including 2017 Special Tony Award for Sound Design, 2017 Drama Desk Outstanding Sound Design in a Play, 2017 Helpmann Award for Best Sound Design and 2016 Evening Standard Award for Best Design.

Joshua Pharo | Lighting & Video Design

Joshua Pharo (he/him) is a lighting designer. Previous theatre credits: *Measure for Measure* (RSC); *Noughts & Crosses* (Regents Park); *The Reckoning* (Arcola); *Kenrex, Contradictions* (Sheffield Theatres); *Stranger Beasts, I Am Kevin, 100: Unearth* (Wildworks); *A Raisin in the Sun, The House Party, Corrina, Corrina* (Headlong); *The Hot Wing King, The Odyssey, Jekyll and Hyde – schools tour* (National Theatre); *Crave, random generations* (Chichester Festival Theatre); *The Human Body, Love and Other Acts of Violence* (Donmar Warehouse); *A Little Princess* (Theatre by the Lake); *A Christmas Carol* (Rose); *Untitled F*ck M*ss S**gon Play, Let the Right One In, Cosmic Scallies, How My Light is Spent* (Royal Exchange); *Wolf Witch Giant Fairy* (Royal Opera House); *Extinct* (Theatre Royal Stratford East); *The Litten Trees* (Fuel); *The Bee in Me* (Unicorn); *Cinderella* (Lyric, Hammersmith); *Going Through* (Bush); *Future Bodies* (HOME); *Nanjing* (Sam Wanamaker Playhouse); *Removal Men* (Yard); *Burning Doors* (Belarus Free); *Bodies* (Royal Court); *The Twits* (Curve). Television credits include: *Where I Go (When I Can't Be Where I Am)* (Rachel Bagshaw/China Plate).

Tom Robbins | Set Design

Tom (he/him) is a Production Manager working across physical and digital spaces to provide technical solutions that facilitate authentic storytelling. For ThickSkin, credits include: *Generator, Driftwood, How Not To Drown* and *Blood Harmony*. Tom has recently worked with companies including National Theatre, Sheffield Theatres, Site Gallery, The University of Sheffield, Sheffield Hallam University, ThickSkin, Common Wealth, Barrel Organ, Cement Fields, Pilot Theatre, Megaverse, RivelinCo, Andro & Eve, Paperfinch Theatre, Roots Mbili Theatre, Migration Matters Festival, Cambridge Literary Festival, Sheaf Poetry Festival, SICK! Festival, WOW! Festival, Estuary.

Madison Omatseone | Design Associate (Costume)

Madison Omatseone (she/her) is a West Yorkshire-based Costume & Set Designer. Madison trained at Rose Bruford College, graduating in 2020. As Associate Designer her recent credits include *Kailey* (Double Jacket Arts/New Wolf Productions). As Assistant Designer: *Public Interest* (Common/Wealth). As Costume Supervisor: *Cinderella* (Cast, Doncaster). For film: *The Woman In Cabin 10,* under triple Academy Award winning costume designer Jenny Beavan, and *Goodbye June* starring Kate Winslet and Helen Mirren (Netflix Originals).

Anna Berentzen | Associate Director

Anna Berentzen (she/her) is ThickSkin's Jerwood Associate Artist, supported by The Jerwood Foundation. Work for ThickSkin: *Pigeon* as Associate Director, and *Generator* as co-Director with Neil Bettles. Other directing credits include: *Leave No Trace, The Tempest* (Buxton Opera House); *A Very Odd Birthday Party* (Hawkseed Theatre, UK Tour); *Astronauts, The Survivors' Guide to Living, All I Want for Christmas* (Royal Exchange Theatre). As Associate or Assistant Director: *Hamlet Hail to the Thief* (RSC and Factory International); *Rumpelstiltskin, Hare & Tortoise* (Buxton Opera House); *In Space R&D* (Ransack, The Lowry, and the National Theatre Studio); *Utopia, The Tempest, We Were Told There Was Dancing, Bruntwood Prize Ceremony* (Royal Exchange Theatre). Anna is Co-Founder of Hawkseed Theatre. She was part of the Royal Exchange Theatre Young Directors' Programme and was later selected to be part of Headlong Origins scheme for regional directors.

Kieran Lucas | Sound Associate

Kieran (he/him) is an award winning sound designer, composer & theatre-maker. Sound & composition credits include: *Me For The World, My Name Is Rachel Corrie* (Young Vic); *First Touch, Noah & The Peacock* (Nottingham Playhouse); *The Legend of Ned Ludd, A Billion Times I Love You* (Liverpool Everyman); *The Marvellous Myth Hunter Ceilidh* (Southbank Centre); *Weather Girl* (St. Anne's Warehouse NYC, Soho Theatre); *Shooting Hedda Gabler, EMMA* (Rose Theatre); *Winter's Tale* (Dailes Teātris, Latvia); *Under The Skin* (St. Paul's Cathedral); *Companion: Moon, How We Save The World* (Natural History Museum); *SHTF* (Schauspielhaus, Vienna); *VL, Black Love, Really Big & Really Loud* (Paines Plough Roundabout); *Square Go* (59E59, NYC); *Hungry, Hear Me Raw* (Soho Theatre); *May Queen* (Belgrade Theatre); *Showdown* (Chamalëon, Berlin); *Chester Mystery Plays* (Chester Cathedral); *Deciphering,*

Antigone, *A Girl In School Uniform [Walks Into A Bar]* (New Diorama Theatre); *The Future Project* (Streatham Space Project); *GASTRONOMIC* (Shoreditch Town Hall, Norwich Theatre Royal); *Found Sound* (Coventry Cathedral); *TBCTV* (Somerset House); *The Drill* (Battersea Arts Centre).

Laura Mallows | Executive Producer

Laura Mallows (she/her) is co-founder and Executive Director of ThickSkin. Laura has executive produced every ThickSkin production since the company's formation. Other credits include, as Producer: *Survivor* (Hofesh Schechter Company), as Associate Producer: *Beautiful Burnout* (Frantic Assembly/National Theatre of Scotland), as General Manager: *Pool (no water)*, *Stockholm* and *Othello* (Frantic Assembly). Laura has also worked for Clean Break, Fifty Nine Productions, Manchester International Festival, Royal Opera House, Shobana Jeyasingh Dance, The Cholmondeleys and The Featherstonehaughs, and the Touring Consortium. She is also an independent arts consultant and a trustee of RTYDS.

Steph Connell | Senior Producer

Steph Connell (she/her) is a freelance Producer working in theatre and events across the UK. As Producer for ThickSkin: *How Not To Drown, Petrichor, Shade, Chalk Farm*, and *The Static*. Steph is also Producer for Sleeping Warrior Theatre Company as well running her own company Steph Connell Productions. Previous roles include Executive Producer for Glasgow-based company Wonder Fools (2018–2024); Artist Development Coordinator at the Tron Theatre; and Stage One Producer at the Citizens Theatre. Steph has also worked for Northern Broadsides, Al Seed Productions, Amy Golding & Hamzeh Hussien, Frantic Assembly, Raw Material, Artichoke, National Theatre of Scotland, Greenwich and Docklands International Festival, Gate Theatre, and the National Centre for Circus Arts.

ThickSkin

Extraordinary stories told in unexpected ways

We are reimagining what theatre can be, telling stories through quality, future-facing, multi-disciplined formats. ThickSkin is helping shape a creative future that is fearless, collaborative, and driven by diverse voices. Our work thrives on throwing doors open, inviting people in, and empowering artists to think big, take risks, and reinvent what is possible.

Established in 2010, ThickSkin has earned a national reputation for bold, high-quality theatre productions blending text, movement and design. The company was founded by Neil Bettles and Laura Mallows who continue to lead the organisation today. We grow and launch exciting new work from our creation space — The Engine Room — in the heart of Wigan, as a launchpad for national and international touring, reaching audiences across the world.

Our work includes a wide range of creative approaches to tell stories in new and inspiring ways. From live stage productions to virtual reality experiences, to immersive audio plays, we make theatre that is rooted in contemporary culture. Through our work, ThickSkin is igniting creativity, raising ambition, and nurturing the next generation of fearless artists.

ThickSkin has a long history of seeking out and supporting new talent, providing meaningful opportunities for collaboration alongside high-calibre creative teams. We nurture talented theatre makers, providing a springboard for artists who are ready to take a leap.

'Manchester-based theatre mavericks'
Creative Tourist

'ThickSkin are well known for pushing the boundaries of theatre'
Theatre South East

For more information visit:
thickskintheatre.co.uk
@thickskintheatre

ThickSkin Team

Artistic Director	Neil Bettles
Executive Producer	Laura Mallows
Head of Marketing & Audiences	Iain Christie
Senior Producer	Steph Connell
Associate Producer	Abi Beaven
Assistant Producer	Rae Bell
Jerwood Associate Artist	Anna Berentzen

Trustees

Inga Hirst (co-Chair), Elizabeth Pickering (co-Chair), George Danczak, Matthew Eames, Gurjinder Singh Kang, Yusuf Khamisa, Verity Overs-Morrell, Michelle Nicholson, Alison Porter.

ThickSkin's work is generously supported by Arts Council England, Backstage Trust, Equity Charitable Trust, Granada Foundation, Jerwood Foundation, John Ellerman Foundation, Three Monkies Trust and Wigan Council.

ThickSkin is the operating name of ThickSkin Theatre, a Registered Charity, no: 1188196. The Engine Room, Trencherfield Mill, Heritage Way, Wigan, WN3 4DL.

Supported using public funding by
ARTS COUNCIL ENGLAND

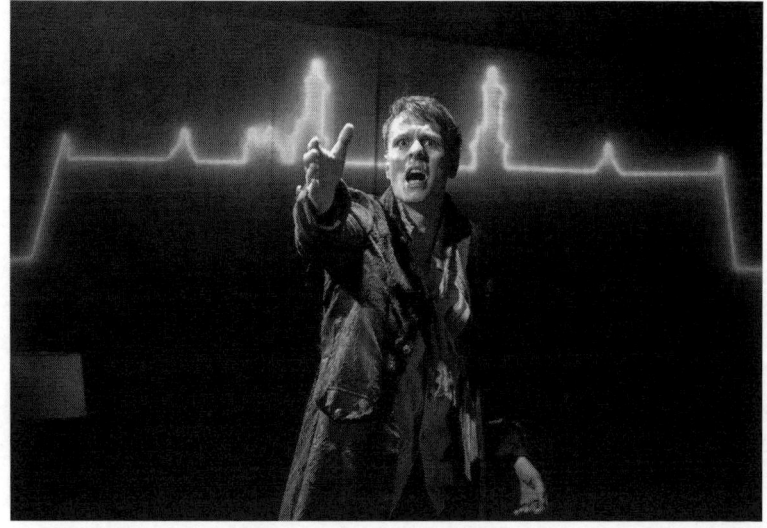

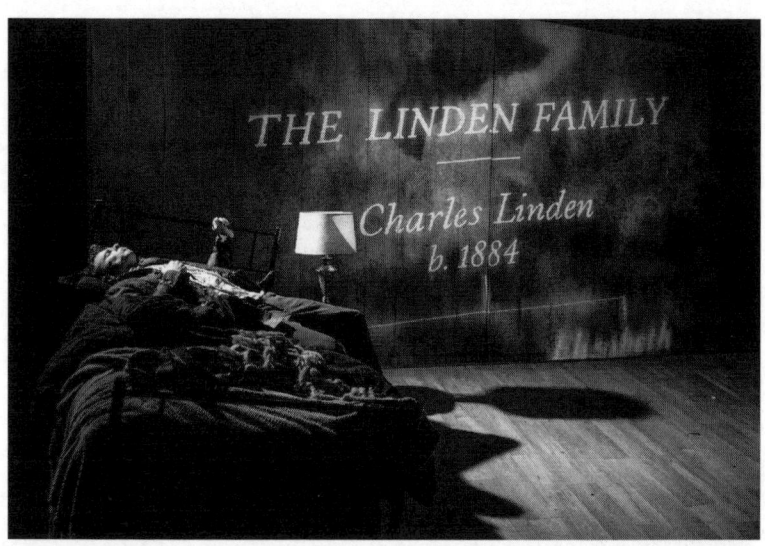

IT WALKS AROUND THE HOUSE AT NIGHT

Characters

JOE
Voice of the OLD MAN
And...?

Setting

The grounds of Paragon Hall.

The Monday to Friday of an October half-term.

Notes

For the text: Speech is to the left, light/sound/action to the right. Commas, dashes, asterisks, ellipses, brackets – all indicators of delivery or pacing. You may decide the rules for yourself.

For the production: This show presents itself as a one-person play. As it descends, we'll see and hear other bodies and voices, especially in the walks and the nightmare sections.

This text went to press before the end of rehearsals and so may differ slightly from the play as performed.

Prologue

> JOE *stands alone.*

He said It walks around the house at night

So I bet like me you're thinking, what

Dead of night, gliding through the rooms, through the walls

Drifting up the stairs, levitating on the landing…?

A grey lady

Or a mad monk

It's got no head

Or it's <u>just</u> a head. Like a really big

Head

Not sure how a head can walk

And the walk is key –

It's the creak of a floorboard

It's the slow *thud, thud, thud*

It's the shadow at the door as the hinges squeeeeak…

And oh my god…

It's a really big head, with legs!

This is wrong, this is. Cos that's not what he meant

It walks around, the house

Like outside. In the grounds. Doesn't come in

It knows its place. And so do I

Out here. In the cold, and the dark, and the rain

On a night-time hike

<u>Five</u> night-time hikes

Through the grounds of Paragon Hall…

I wanna make this clear before we begin

I wanna warn you

And not just about the cold, and the dark, and the rain

'It Walks Around The House At Night'

So you're gonna walk it with me

Are you ready?

Monday

You need to know the route

Cos I had to know the route too, very precise

You leave the lodge and the ghost walk starts by the 'kitchen garden'

(Walled-off bit, full of herbs, all dead by now)

You walk directly towards the house – not that you see it yet

The view's obscured by big trees and the old stables –

But you know it's there, this great big, looming thing

Like you <u>feel</u> it

Keep heading straight until you come to a messy hedge

This circles the house and the lawn. Turn right, follow the hedge around

And you enter, at the bottom, the miniature woodland

Spoilers, not that miniature

Gonna be muddy so be careful

But it curves up, and up

And you're on a raised bit and the trees pull back like stage curtains

There it is

Paragon Hall…

Follow the path back down into the trees again, this is the densest bit

But it's downhill so you feel all, I dunno, lighter

Hedge reappears on the left, stick with it, not far now, lil further…

Kitchen garden. That's the ghost walk, sorted

Takes about twenty-five minutes, and you never get too close to the house

David said that'd give the game away

I was scheduled to do this walk at ten o'clock each night

Course, when we tested it out, it was broad daylight

Strolling around with David Linden, Lord of the Manor…

You don't know David

Neither did I, not really

He was a regular at the bar I work at, you give them all nicknames

'Chardonnay Sharon', 'Tommy Two Pints'

Usually something to do with their order

Or it's a warning. 'Mr Grabby', 'Diarrhoea Debbie'

But David, he was a class above, he was

'The Handsome Stranger'

I came up with that. Had the look of a film star, or an old-timey actor

Now if he'd really been an actor, like moi, would've hated him, but he wasn't, so I didn't

Never Date an Actor

That's up there with Never Date a Colleague

Trust me: I broke both those rules with Dufus, guy who worked part-time

Who was an Adonis, but also, obviously, a-Dufus

Getting sidetracked – David

Promise you, I didn't know he was rich at first

Maybe I guessed – the suit, the skin, the hair

Rich stuff always has a, sheen

We chatted, you know, the odd flirty remark

But the night everything changed –

I was lighting the candles in the beer garden

This was my responsibility ever since I'd sent Dufus out to do it

Said he could use the blowtorch from the kitchen

And he set one of the parasols on fire

Honestly, such a Dufus –

Anyway, it was the first cold night of the year

Like it was September, but it was cold

David's out here, alone

Sitting in the dark and watching me

I make my way around the tables

Snaking towards him in a sexy kinda way…

Wasn't sexy at all, after what, eight hours, no break

Scrubbing up some vom in one of the bogs

(We were just thankful that Diarrhoea Debbie wasn't in that night)

I get close enough to David, I can feel how cold he is

I wanna, I dunno, tell him to come inside, it's too chilly for him out here

But he speaks first:

I have a job for you

Oh here we go

So I lean in close

And David tells me what he wants from me

He wants me to… be a ghost

Okay?

So he has this house in the countryside

And he has his two nieces staying over at half-term

He's told them all about a spook that wanders around the house

And he wants to hire someone to play the part

I'd talked to him a bit about my acting work, so…

Three things I latch onto:

First, 'house in the countryside', hello

Second – 'nieces' – not his own kids, that's good as well

I cast him in my head as 'fun gay uncle'

Third, and this is the best one – this is what I needed to hear –

He remembered I was an actor

Trying to be

Was actually thinking of giving up

All that month I'd. Wasn't in a great place

The whole Dufus break-up, I was fresh out of that

There'd been this really big theatre rejection, don't get me started

And I was in a teensy bit of debt that was, you know, angry email stage

So I was getting out of it, the industry, the bar, the everything

Time for a proper job. Something with a tie

But David's here and he's telling me he'll put me up for the week

Cover my expenses

Then he tells me the fee

I nearly knock over his drink:

Two thousand pounds?

He's wondering if that's enough and I'm like

That's enough

I book the week off work as soon as I get back inside

Go out that night to celebrate. I spend way too much, but who cares –

Two thousand pounds! For a week's acting!

For a jolly in the countryside!

With David...

> JOE *gets into his costume.*

He picked me up from Hexley Station

Showed me the walk, then took me to my digs

The lodge, it's on the grounds and it looks the part –

Stone, thatch, roses growing up the wall, like something on a tin in a charity shop

Inside is... it's fine

I am a little disappointed I won't stay in the actual house

But I can't, not with the nieces, that <u>would</u> give the game away

Sharing a bathroom with the ghost outside, hiya. (Boo)

Hey, maybe David wants to use me as an excuse to get away from them

I ask how old the kids are, I think he said seven and eight before?

But he doesn't wanna talk about that –

He walks to the fridge and opens it with a flourish

It is full, to the brim, with the most expensive shit

All from farmers' markets

Pops a bottle of prosecco

Pours me a glass

We make a toast to our haunting

Shame I can't stick around, he says

And he looks at me with those heavenly grey eyes...

I'm checking him out as he walks back down the path

Yeah we are absolutely gonna –

> JOE*'s phone buzzes.*

(Fuck off)

Gabby

Texting about the Wednesday delivery

I wanna text back saying 'I do not care'…

But I don't cos I'm terrified of her

Gabby, she's the bar manager

I'm the assistant manager

Which means she makes me her lil bitch

And I spread that bitching out to everyone else

She's annoyed I'm away this week

I'm meant to get time off for acting work, I'd reminded her of that –

But she said this wasn't an actual job

I was only doing this to have sex with David. Which absolutely wasn't, a lie

I send her pics of the bedroom to annoy her even more

Then a selfie of me in costume

This was all laid out for me

Like I say costume but it's really old

Probably real-life period clothing

Like Georgian, or Victorian, or – I dunno I did Geography

Gabby fails to give me an appropriate compliment

Instead she's zoomed in and screenshotted the view outside the bedroom window

What building is that, she asks

Paragon Hall, I reply

*

I know I haven't described it yet?

The house

I just feel a, in my chest a…

> *A strange heartbeat…*
>
> *…that fades away.*

Black and white

Tudor, maybe, it's all criss-cross with wood beams and mortar and

Okay it's old, that's all you've gotta –

Like it's always been there

Like this ancient valley fucking howled

And spat out a house

It's only as I watch the sun set on that massive fucking thing

That I realise how mad it is

Somebody owns that

Lives in that

All by himself

Is he, by himself? I get the vibe

He's never mentioned a partner, I was on high alert for that

Maybe he has an ancient aunt, like Maggie Smith

She's a hundred but comes out with all these catty remarks

Oh, maybe she knew the ghost I'm meant to –

> *Knock at the door interrupts.*

David returns

I smile at my Handsome Stranger…

But he doesn't smile back

Like, he smiles, but I can tell it isn't a real smile

He's nervous… and I'm thinking that's sweet, that's really sweet

He wants this to go well

He's changed his suit

Not in his normal style, it's a black-and-white three-piece

Like he's matching the house

Are you ready?

My five-minute call. Hang on, is it nearly ten o'clock?

Only now do I see how dark it's got

Night hasn't just fallen, it's squished everything around us

I check the time and I say something like you bet, or let's go

But he nods at the phone in my hand and says

You can't take that

And I feel pretty silly cos yeah

A Victorian ghost –

Or Georgian, whatever –

Wouldn't be scrolling through their socials

                                      JOE *throws his phone away.*

All set

Before he leaves me, David reminds me of the rules:

Stick to the route

Don't double-back

And never, ever, approach the house

The First Walk

How's a ghost meant to walk?

I'd been wondering that

Can't even see where my feet touch the floor, not yet, my eyes need to

I've never known a dark like it

The path from the kitchen garden to the hedge felt like nothing in the light –

Here, it's stretching, and I'm stumbling and…

A faint shudder in the air

Like a breeze or, I dunno

It's nippy out here, need to move to keep warm

I know David won't want me rushing it

But I find myself speeding up slightly

Getting a bit of a strut on

It's fine, he's just that kind of ghost

My hand's doing this, thing

Twitching

Even without my phone, it's trying to scroll, the ghost of a phone

Have to hold my hand to make it still

It's nerves of course, I dunno why

Maybe cos I haven't acted in a while?

Not that this is really acting…

I mean I'm acting a little bit, I'm acting all calm –

Cos as I brush along the hedge, I have a silly thought

One of those silly thoughts you shouldn't think cos then you can't stop thinking it:

I wonder if I'm the only ghost out here tonight

I am not, superstitious

I do not believe in ghosts

David asked me that when he gave me the job and I laughed

But on this walk

This first walk…

No I still don't, course I don't –

But I'd swear there was…

Something?

No

Something behind me?

As I'm coming into the woods

As I slow my steps, as the path changes shape

The sound of my footsteps don't keep in time with me

Like there are more, footsteps, behind me…?

A weird echo

The way the trees line the path, the shards of darkness

Doing something funny with the sound

Cos the sound, is me, I'm just being silly

And to prove that, I'm gonna stop

JOE stops.

And turn around…

Beat.

There's nothing there.

Hope the nieces can't see me yet

Not sure a ghost should be scared of other –

Jumpscare. (A bat flaps by.)

JOE *recovers.*

The path's getting steeper

We're nearing the bit where I'm gonna see the house

Where I'll be the most exposed –

I force myself to slow right down

As I enter stage left

Looking down on Paragon Hall…

But it feels like it's, looking down on me

Like the night made the land all fluid and everything's the wrong height

The white of the house stands out, half-sketched

But all the lights are off

I guess the nieces need it dark inside, to see better outside

And David wouldn't let them use the big light

(No self-respecting gay can use the big light)

So I take a moment, stand there

Breathing

Floating…

Yeah and now I really need to keep walking

Downhill, getting faster. Why am I getting faster?

I can pretend the speed isn't me, just gravity, but no

No I'm speeding up cos I'm definitely being followed

Don't just hear it now, I know it, I feel it –

A heaviness behind me

A whisper, barely audible: (Don't turn around.)

I'm ignoring it

But my head is rattling with nonsense:

If there's life out here, there's death out here –

I'm nearly out of the woods, nearly, nearly

I feel a breeze behind me

But it's not a breeze, it's something, breathing out –

Reaching out – a silhouette, rising –

I am freaking – faster, faster

The trees fall away but they're also falling towards me

And the path's all muddy and I'm slipping and I'm bigger bigger strides and I'm fuck!

David!

We're back by the kitchen garden and he's holding a… lantern?

He looks at me with his big wide eyes

But it's not like before, the smile is

It's real this time. Happy, ecstatic

He asks me how I found the walk –

Whispers it, like it's something sacred –

And I dunno what to say

Nothing at first

I ask him if the girls had fun

Let's walk you home. Stay close

His sheen is back. He glistens in the bad light

Warm, sweaty… like he ran out here to meet me

And the path to the lodge, the crunch of the gravel

Getting further from the house, the walk, all those silly things I –

David's hand brushes against mine

It's hot

Like there's heat coming off it

But it's hot in other ways too

*

We reach the lodge

I try to ask him in

But I can't say anything, my throat's too dry

And David's already walking back into the night

I close the door

I lock it tight

I'm safe in here, I'm safe

I'm gonna sleep well tonight

*

<u>The First Nightmare</u>

Darkness.

Streaks of light appear and disappear.

Within them, JOE *is suspended in different spaces, different shapes.*

At one point it looks like he's trying to escape.

He's alone, he's alone, he's alone… except for when he isn't.

Tuesday

'Your house doesn't exist'

I'm groggy and I'm aching and I'm looking at this text and

Yeah no idea what Gabby's on about

She sent it late, probably drunk. I don't reply

Slept in late today

I squint outside, in case Gabby is right, if the house vanished in the night…

Still there

And in the morning grey it looks, I dunno

I google it

'Paragon Hall'

Wondering if there's anything about the history, if they ever used it for filming

Maybe I'll even find the story of my ghost

But there's nothing here, nothing about the house at all

One of those places that can afford to be private

So I find myself googling more familiar territory

'David Linden'

I did this all the time on my breaks at the bar

He's a trustee for a big firm in Manchester

And he's got his sexy headshot

Not that I need it, I can picture him instantly…

The cruder among you will be thinking

'He's lying in bed, thinking of his future lover, we all know what he's gonna do' –

You're filthy, you should be ashamed of yourself

And you're absolutely right

Except I couldn't, cos my hand – both my hands now –

Weirdly in pain

I get this flash of my grandad's fingers

Those claws of sandpaper he used to hold in his lap, which gave him so much agony –

But I need to stop thinking about him

Cos grandads, and morning wood, horrific combination

Right above the fireplace is this massive oil painting of a young man

A Victorian gentleman

(And I know he's Victorian cos the Victorians were sad and this one's miserable)

But the more I look at it, the more I know, I just, know…

This is my ghost

This is who I'm dressing up as

I mean he doesn't look anything like me

He's smaller, gaunter, paler

But the outfit's the same

And I feel a – it's a melancholy –

Like he knows he's dead already

Name at the bottom:

'Charles Linden'

Well, talking of grandads –

Or like, great-great-grandads –

This is one of David's lot

Don't see the resemblance

I look around for more family pictures –

I head to the windowsill to see if –

Jumpscare. (*A face appears.*)

Fuck!

There's a guy outside!

He's gone

Fuck, it was this old guy, and he was looking

Wrong

No, no no no, just the gardener or something

In a new place, bound to be jumpy

Just some passer-by

*

It gets dark too fast again

I doomscroll the day away

Gabby keeps texting

Asking if I'd met her new girlfriend, Andrea

I hadn't, and I didn't want to

I text back something bland

'Has Dufus set anything on fire again'

Okay his name wasn't actually Dufus, do I really need to – ?

Rufus

Slumming it with the rest of us, but secretly, rather posh

Don't know if it <u>was</u> a secret actually

Always so flush with cash, buying everybody drinks

Oh, and there was that time he had a bit-part on *Bridgerton*

And the guy who owned the house they filmed in turned out to be a cousin so

Yeah he was posh

Yes he was on *Bridgerton*, yes he was getting more acting gigs than me

No I wasn't jealous, that's not why we, broke up

I mean it didn't help

He was always buying me gifts, treating me to dinner, it was insufferable

Then he'd been all sweet and understanding about my big theatre rejection…

Could've throttled him

Couldn't throttle anyone now, my hands are still

And there's a knot in my stomach

With the last of the light

It's coming back

The dread

Knock at the door. a little louder.

Are we ready?

David has the wrong smile again

I wish he'd wear another suit

Looks like he's going to a bloody funeral

The Second Walk

Cloudier tonight

Even in the black you can see the sky has curdled

Moonlight burping from behind the mess

Colder too. Or is it?

As I walk towards the hedge, there's a warm breeze pushing through it

Rustling. Like something's, lying in wait…

No, I gotta snap out of this

Okay, look, I may have done a bad thing

I may have brought my phone

Nobody can see my airpods from this far away

I just think a bit of music, will help me relax

Character research:

What does my Victorian ghost like to listen to?

An inappropriate song plays: modern and jaunty.

He's a modern Victorian

JOE *walks to the tune for a bit. Maybe starts to dance.*
Then he takes one headphone out and the music becomes tinny.

Getting closer to the trees

This is where I heard it before

The figure, following

I tread as quietly as I can

And I listen

Half to the music, half to…

If there's anything else

But there's no footsteps behind me

Can't even hear my own this time

Like I'm gliding over black silk…

> *The music starts to warp.*

Like the land is, changing shape…

And I'm looking down and I, this is so stupid –

I think I've, fallen over?

It's not rough or muddy or anything

It's freezing, it's

Nothing

I'm hanging in nothing

And I'm panicking, I'm

My heart is pounding, pounding –

> *The music returns to normal..*

Fucking, music's fucking distracting me

> JOE *pulls out his other headphone. The music stops.*

Freaking myself out

I can't do this, I can't – have a heart attack out here, dressed like this

I'd become the ghost for real!

Let's get this bloody job over with

*

There's a little more light in the windows tonight

And maybe that's a figure, a shadow on the glass…

But as I'm staring at the house, the dark around me's getting

Less dark?

It's, uh, green?

An eerie green

It must be a trick of the light – but why's there any light to trick me?

I step back in the trees

Smeared over the roots…

The floor is shimmering, blistering

Is it moss, or

No

Mushrooms

So, many, mushrooms, glowing, what?

Speckled with this, sickly neon

Flinching with it

I can't work out if it's disgusting or if it's beautiful

Probably both

I kinda, wanna lie down in it, is that weird?

That's weird

I go to touch the nearest one…

But wait I need a picture of this. I reach for my

Phone

No

Shit

Dropped my phone

Not out here, shit

Already I'm retracing my steps, I could've dropped it anywhere, I could've dropped it –

Oh, there

I'm thinking how much worse that could've been

As JOE *picks up his phone...*

My neck prickles

I crouch very still

And I realise what I've done

I've doubled-back

And whatever

Was following me...

Is now right in front of me

A silhouette, rising...

*

Running fuck fuck running

Spinning through the woods

Branches whipping past, scratching, grabbing

Not gonna stop

Cos that thing is

Oh my God oh my God

Not gonna stop

There's a light up ahead

A light at the end of the path and it's there, it's there, it's

David again! David David David

I collapse into his arms

But he pushes me back

He's saying, something, can't hear him, I'm too

Blood thumping in my ears

I take a deep breath

Look at him properly

Why are you running?

He's angry

I try to say there's something following me, I'm pointing down the path –

Empty

I look at David

He looks at me

Does he think I'm mad? I'm about to tell him about the old man this morning –

But he grabs my wrist

Tight

He yanks it up

My phone

He's seen my phone

He's gripping so tight

He's hurting me

*

Walk back

Silence

I don't look back as I enter the lodge

My mind, raging

What the fuck is – what the fuck was tonight –

I stumble through the cottage

Lungs heavy, eyes burning –

I'm gonna cry

I'm texting, someone, I'm texting David

My thumbs are in agony

'I can't do this', I type

Even sign it with a kiss

I collapse on the bed in costume

I'm gonna leave first thing

*

<u>The Second Nightmare</u>

JOE *is in bed.*

The fridge opens, glowing white.

He gets up, slowly approaches…

Closes it.

JOE *goes back to bed.*

The fridge opens, this time glowing green, full of rotting mushrooms.

JOE *sits up in bed…*

The fridge slams shut.

He gets up, slowly approaches…

Opens the fridge. The normal white inside.

JOE *goes back to bed.*

The fridge bursts open and a shadow scuttles out of it.

JOE *leaps out of bed to face it.*

There's nothing in front of him.

It's behind him. 'Don't turn around.'

Wednesday

Why do ghosts stick around?

Some say it's cos they hurt so much

I think it's out of spite

*

Seven missed calls

One long voicenote

David

I must be hungover, did something stupid…

Then it all comes flooding back

Nope, not listening to that, not yet

Roll out of bed. Afternoon already

Bar work messes with your body clock but this is something else

I stagger to the bathroom for a piss, stare at my reflection –

Fuck me. Rough

Eyes, bloodshot. And my skin looks like it's been…

That thing in the forest

It wasn't the man from the garden before, wasn't a man at all –

I was tripping, okay, those mushrooms, their spores, the twinkly, I dunno

Panic. Just, panic

I slump back on the bed and press play

I expect David to be angry

But… he's not, he's sweet

He's so apologetic about how he was last night

Inexcusable, can't say sorry enough

And he totally understands if I wanna step away from the job

But if I stick around he's prepared to

Up my fee?

No

What?

I scroll the voicenote back

Did he say

And he says it again:

Ten thousand pounds

Ten thousand pounds?

Ten thousand pounds

Ten thousand – I'm playing it a few times to make sure

Ten thousand pounds, wow

That's insane

That is insane

And suddenly all my worries from last night, gone

Cos there is a lot I will put up with, for ten fucking grand

That's life-changing

That's like, debt-free

Or I focus on my show!

I was working on a play? Like, tryna write it, act it

About my grandad, actually

And there was a big theatre, my local theatre –

Where Mum took me to see my first panto –

They were gonna help me make this play

Incredible

Being backed like that. Being a part of that

My, theatre. Telling my, story…

…but my story wasn't quite what they were after:

He's a little angry. It's a bit much

And I suggest well actually, considering what he put up with

How he was physically broken, how he dropped dead before his pension…

Maybe he wasn't angry enough?

That shut them up

Like, that really shut them up –

The emails went quiet, the contract never arrived –

I was starting to get, you know

But Dufus was convinced it'd all work out for me

Cos it turns out, his dad – who is a baron by the way, an actual baron –

Well, he's on the board of the theatre

Makes a lot of donations

He's a powerful man, he can pull some strings

So, if I wanna meet him, if I wanna ask him for some help…

Dufus doesn't get why that makes me even angrier

Like he thinks I'm not good enough to get this gig on my own

Fuck you Dufus, I'm gonna put in the effort, and they're gonna put on my play!

Twist in the tale, they don't

They drop me. And rejection…

Come on, by this point, I don't know anything else

Ten thousand pounds, nah, not wasting that on a failed play

Gonna go to Mykonos or something

*

First thing I do is drop Gabby a text and say 'I quit'

Followed by 'lol jokes'

Followed by 'no but I'm getting 10k now so not gonna work for a while byeee'

She's typing back…

JOE's phone buzzes.

Okay, she's ignored my mini retirement

All she says is:

'Andrea's gonna give you a call'

*

Paragone Hall

Originally with an 'e' at the end of the name

The estate was granted in the twelve-hundreds to a Sir Thomas Something, before passing in marriage a century later to the Linden family. The house itself dates from the late sixteenth century, that's the distinctive Tudor style – see I guessed it was Tudor – and modifications were made in the nineteenth century, including a garden design in homage to the deity Pan. But the house fell into disrepair when the final Linden, a Charles Linden, died a few weeks before Queen Victoria in 1901. It was torn down five years later

*

I'm standing in my boxers, having a posh coffee

As I listen to this potted history of the house

It's being delivered in an uninterrupted monologue by Andrea

This is not who I imagined Gabby with at all

She's like, a nerd? Full-on history buff

She did say what her PhD was in but I wasn't listening

Andrea finishes her spiel and I point out there are a couple of mistakes

First being, the house wasn't pulled down, I'm looking at it right now

Unless David rebuilt it. Which is my second point –

All the Lindens can't be dead

I'm trying to hook up with one

But Andrea's adamant

She's even made some academic calls –

The Lindens, are absolutely gone

And she ought to know, cos she's been researching them for a while

This is when someone grabs the phone off Andrea

Starts ranting in Spanish

It's Gabby, going off on one

English words start poking through

She's making it clear that she never liked this David

The Handsome Stranger with the devil eyes

She says she'll tell me what her girlfriend won't –

That Andrea's been keeping tabs on him

This is why they met in the first place, she came into the bar one night and –

Hang on, what? What are you on about?

Gabby doesn't actually know what David's up to but it's no good, no es bueno

Don't care if it's bueno, I say

He's giving me ten grand

She swears again. Tells me that amount of money won't do anything

Not in this economy

If I'm gonna sell my soul, why do I have to be so cheap?

'Cheap'

So

I tell her, what I think of her shitty little bar

Always smelling of sweat, and sick

What I think of her as well

That she's old, washed-up, bitter

And all her dreams have fucking, rotted away

And the worse thing is, so have mine, yeah? So I fucking deserve, a break

Right. Well

Guess I don't work for Gabby any more

Knock on the door. Even louder than before.

Can't be time already

Nah it's not. It's later than I think but it's not

I start to worry about the creepy gardener...

But it's David again

Early. Standing there all foppish

Like Hugh Grant on my doorstep

Holding a wicker basket, asking if I got his messages

If I can possibly make it up to you

The icy blast reminds me that I'm standing here

In my boxers

I smile at David

He smiles back

Are we gonna…

Get dressed

But there's a twinkle in his eye

Cos we're going for a picnic

*

I've had champagne before

Working at functions

Wearing silly suits, sneaking off with spare bottles

But this stuff, I will never forget the taste

The label was dusty

He pours it into a china cup. I press the cold against my lips and sip

The bubbles, like butter

The sweetness, like, flowers that had all died out

There are sandwiches and little cakes and

The posher food gets, the smaller it is and I love it

We're round the other side of the hall

There's a lake I haven't seen, at the bottom of a dip

And we sit on the grass, our backs to the house

Looking over the water. Daylight dancing on the surface

And all the horrors of night feel so far away

David makes a point of asking about my family –

I talk of the struggles with my mum

She's in a bit of a mess, she's about to be evicted

Then I realise I'm not spending that ten grand on a holiday am I

I have to help her. And that makes me, angry

I don't wanna talk about my family any more, I wanna talk about David's

The portrait in the lodge, I say, he's a relative of yours

David doesn't say anything

He just stares across the lake...

Like I still wanna fancy him

My wrist is bruised, but I pull down my sleeve

Cos things would be so much easier if it's me and him and picnics

He wants me acting, he's paying for me, investing in me –

His hand brushes up against my knee

I'm ready for this, I'm so ready

I lean in

But then I ruin it, I absolutely –

Cos for some reason I find myself saying

I hope the nieces aren't watching!

Like, that'd kill the mood anyway

But I see a familiar flicker in his eyes

That I've seen on stage when someone's forgotten their lines...

And that is when I know, when it is absolutely clear to me

There are no nieces

This man is lying to me...

He pulls away as it starts spitting rain. *It's late*

I'm a little, I dunno, stunned, I dunno what to do

I start packing up the hamper so I don't have to look at him

But he stops me. A cold hand on mine

It's late, he says again

And off he strides, up to the house, doesn't look back

I sit here by a wreck of a picnic

Rain's getting heavier

All this wasted food

And my stomach's getting twisted again

I hurry to the lodge, start getting ready –

Sorry, what the fuck am I doing?

Who the fuck am I doing it for?

If there aren't any nieces – no, but there was someone watching, at the window

David? Or the guy I saw? Or is he the one following me? If he isn't, who is? What is?

Where's my phone? Did I leave it on charge? I need to check it, can't find it –

Gonna have to go, gonna have to go, gonna have to –

> *Knock at the door. The loudest yet.*

Ten thousand pounds

It's worth it

The Third Walk

This walk's different from the get-go

It's not the cold or the rain –

It's the champagne

I'm tipsy, I'll admit it

Yeah and it's making me reckless, as drink always does

Tonight I am gonna find out who's following me

I am finding out tonight

Fuck this shit, you know? I'm not a coward

I don't believe in ghosts, I really don't

Cos whoever is creeping up on me

Flesh and blood

And I can take flesh and blood, I can –

Hear him

Okay

Okay

Head down

Keep walking

I know what I'm gonna do

I know where I'm gonna do it

When the hedge becomes the wood, there's a bit of the path I can dart down, crouch

Then I'll see the fucker that's, that's…

Okay, this is bonkers

But there's something about the footsteps tonight

The lumbering, rambling

Doesn't sound as horrifying as before

Maybe he wants to get out of the rain and all

So just before I reach the trees – I dart, I duck

I wait

Waiting

Getting closer

Haven't thought what I'll do when he gets here

Gabby always has a baseball bat behind the bar

Maybe there's a branch, or a –

But I see him

A figure in the dark

And my stomach just – fuck it –

*

I realise something's wrong

When the figure squeals

It's a familiar squeal

Dufus?!

He gives me his, goofy grin

His white teeth bright in the night

What the hell are you doing here!

He says *I come when I'm called*, and I say well I didn't call

And he says *no buddy, but you did text me*

I hate it when he calls me buddy. And I <u>didn't</u> text him

But he doesn't care, he's just happy to be here

Didn't have any shifts for a couple of days and Hexley wasn't far

So you've been following me every night, I say

That is the creepiest thing to do to an ex

But he gives me a look, shakes his head –

Only just got here buddy

And I really don't wanna believe him

Cos at this point I am desperate for something, rational, even if it isn't

But then back along the walk

We hear this, cry

Like a fox or a child or a –

> *An unearthly cry.*

I pull Dufus down the path

Keep hold of his hand, for his sake not mine

And into the woods we go

He has no idea what's happening

But I'm reassuring him and I'm feeling brave again

Cos looking after someone so, clueless

It's kinda, comforting

I'm gripping his hand and I'm telling him move, keep moving –

But he's slowing down

Smiling in the green light. All drowsy, like he's just, woken up

He points to the fungus, scattered around the floor

And he tells me it's foxfire

That's the name, foxfire, it's the light

From the fungi

Bioluminescence

And then suddenly it's like the night stops –

> *Everything stops.*
>
> *The world twinkles green.*

And he tells me a story of him and his dad, one night on their estate. Standing in an orchard, in a twilight green like this. He'd never been close to his dad, but tonight felt different. Cos they were sharing this wonder. His dad explained how the fungus broke down the dead and made new life, made this light. And that made Rufus think of his mum, who he'd lost when he was young. They'd scattered her ashes in the fields of their house. Maybe she was in this shine, this glow…

And it's a beautiful story

But I'm not hearing any of it

I'm hearing 'orchard', 'estate'

I'm hearing him talk about his dad, the baron

The one who never approved of us, the one who, who…

I don't wanna think of that now –

I just wanna think of Rufus, in this moment, his joy, his smile

The boy who came all this way to hold my hand

But he's slipping out of reach

That gap between us, getting wider and wider and –

The night starts up again.

I see a light on the path ahead – the lantern again

That's David, coming to find me, how long have we been – shit

I tell Dufus to hide, but he's already –

Where's? No time to look for him

The Handsome Stranger arrives

Looking scared

You're really late tonight

I decide on my excuse

Give a little wobble –

I've acted drunk before –

David grabs me by the jacket, pulls me down the hill

I can see from the way he's refusing to look at me, look at anything

He knows something's out here

He's been sending me on these walks and he

I'm angry

I'm angry and I should say something

But I don't

I'm thinking about Dufus back there…

*

Back at the lodge

David on the doorstep, dusting off my jacket

Making out he was only rushing back to get me out the rain

And I just have this, face

Same face when I'm dealing with a shitty customer

I'm thinking, you bastard

We had a picnic today and we nearly made out and you're a bastard

I fake a yawn, time for bed

And close the door

I switch on the light –

Oh. I try all the lights

(Yes, even the big light)

Has the power gone?

Doesn't matter – need to find my phone, find my phone –

Messages from Gabby –

Not bothering with those right now –

Messages from Dufus…

And he was right. I had texted him

In the haze of last night. Begging him to come rescue me

And of course he did: 'Hey buddy, don't worry, I'm driving down now'

I do use him. I keep, using him…

I lied before

I did take that meeting, with his dad

Met the noble baron to ask about the big theatre, his theatre

Ask if he could help me

The way he smirked

How he told me, he'd been meaning to have a word

He knew about me and his son

He knew about the presents, and the restaurants, and the loans

And he didn't like his boy hanging out with someone so, cheap

So he offered me a 'gentleman's agreement'

If I left his boy. If I stopped using him

He would put in a good word for me, with the theatre

And I, did it, I dumped him

And a week later my play was official cancelled, so

Now he's out there, in the dark…

*

As I go to find Dufus, I give him a call

He'll stay round here tonight, he's not driving back

He doesn't answer

I try him again, and again

I'm trying him for the seventh, eighth time –

> *Thud.*
>
> *Beat.*
>
> *Another thud.*

Someone's back in the lodge

Did Dufus…? Maybe he slipped past me

But how did he know where –

> *Thud.*
>
> JOE *re-enters the lodge.*

Rufus?

> *Silence.*
>
> JOE *puts on the torch of his phone.*
>
> *Creak.*
>
> JOE *pans the torch around… but there's nothing…*
>
> *Still nothing. Until –*
>
> *'Don't turn around.'*
>
> *A shape appears! The torch goes out –*
>
> JOE *is grabbed by the dark.*

The Warning

> *As the light changes,* JOE *steps out of the story.*
> *An audio recording of the* OLD MAN *begins to play.*
> *A* DANCER *moves around the space, bringing it to life.*

*

It walks around the house at night…

And so did I.

I was a dancer. When I lived in Manchester. Trying to be.

Classes in the day, nights I worked in a burger bar.

David Linden ate here. Out-of-place, a shiny man in a grubby booth. But he looked kind. He tipped well. Said he knew I was a dancer, the way I moved…

Then one night he said he wanted to hire me. He was entertaining guests for a week – a sister and a nephew from America, keen to experience an English haunting. He wanted to give them a ghost. I thought that was cute. I thought he was cute too.

What followed that week is what's happening to you now.

A succession of evening walks that got darker, stranger. At night there were violent dreams, the next day my body would be flooded with aches and pains. The hours of light whipped by so fast and soon all I was doing was this job, this damn job, going round and round. I constantly felt a panic or a stage fright, as though something was pursuing me, waiting in the wings, ready to devour me whole.

I was a dancer, I knew how to smile through the pain.

It got me on the fourth night.

I thought I knew the route by now, but as soon as I entered the woods the path began to coil and twist like it was trying to throw me off. By now I wasn't so steady on my feet, but I ran through the forest. I heard It behind me. It was getting closer and closer –

And my ankle snapped.

I fell to the ground in agony. And something… pulled me up. Its jaws were the night…

…and I woke up in the lodge and I had no idea what was going on. But David was here. Dabbing the cuts and scratches on my face. I was too sick to speak, but he knew there was only one thing I'd ask:

What was that thing?

And he told me. This was a secret he'd carried for so long, it was bursting out of him.

There once was a time when the Linden line looked set to end. The final heir, the young Charles Linden, was a sickly boy, not long for this world. If he were lost, a great family of England would fall. That couldn't be allowed to happen.

The Lindens owned a great deal of land, but they owned more than that – the very power of the land. So an impossible deal was struck. He didn't say how it was made, or who it was with. He only spoke of a trick. But from the way he described this ancient force that roamed the hillside and defied the laws of nature… I thought of a ballet I was in as a kid. When we danced with the Great God Pan.

The deal was this: Charles Linden would be given five more years. He would be kept alive, continue to rule his countryside. But when this was done… Then It would come. Over five nights, It would take Its time, It would take Its toll.

The Lindens said they agreed to the terms.

They did not.

That dreaded week arrived. But instead of giving up the boy, David's forebears fought back. First they hired cunning folk to banish the creature, but their charms didn't hold. Then they used force, tried to physically restrain the beast… but those unlucky enough to bar Its way were lost to the woods forever.

Finally, they came up with a ploy. They dressed a servant as the master of the house… they filled him with rich foods, made him stroll the grounds… They gave It a waif and stray that wouldn't be missed.

And it worked. So now they knew:

To buy the Lindens time, they could feed It scraps.

The following year It came again, so next was the stable boy.

A year after that, the apprentice from the blacksmith's. Then

a lad from the village over, further, further, more, more…

So this was David's job. It was something his dad had done and his dad before. He was to find young men, young healthy men,

who had slipped through the cracks, to walk the grounds of Paragon Hall. They were needed when the veil between worlds was thin. When the creature returned, when the tithe was due.

It was now David leaned in to remind me: I still had a job to do.

They owed It one more night.

I laughed. Or I shrieked, I can't remember. Shouting, swearing, wouldn't do it, couldn't do it! But David said I would walk as

agreed or my family would suffer.

David left at dusk. My fever spiking, my ankle swollen, my

nerves shredded. I wept.

And then I walked around the house again.

Sometimes I convince myself I don't remember. The way

I hobbled and howled, the way It hunted me down...

I have no idea how I survived. But I lost so much. If you see me now – and you have, seen me now, you were terrified when you glimpsed me in the garden – I am old, withered, twisted...

This house, these grounds, that family – they bled me dry. They took my youth and my life. And still the creature hungers...

It becomes clear this audio is from JOE*'s phone.*

I didn't want to return, but I felt I. To see David's latest victim.

To see you. I don't know if I can help you. I've scared you again tonight. Maybe I should've waited until you were awake, tell you my story face-to-face. But you needed to rest, the walks take it out of you. And I... I don't want to be remembered like this.

I leave you my warning.

Now it's up to you...

Thursday

> JOE *puts the phone away.*

I've never been in shock before

If that's what this is

Feels like doing an all-nighter, being kind of

Numb, but knowing you have to

Carry on, or you're just gonna…

He's saying, It's really out there

There's a thing that's coming for me, draining me…

I play the recording on my phone again. And again, till the sun comes up

Now I, uh, have to act, yeah

First thing I do is leave the lodge

It's different at dawn, misty, empty

I hurry to the bit in the woods where I'd left him

Rufus

Still isn't answering his phone

I'm ringing and I'm ringing and

Maybe this isn't where I left him, can't see any mushrooms –

But I find it

His phone

On the ground

And nearby

Is a dark patch

Where the earth has been

Scorched

In the shape of a, a

Body?

I'm shaking. And then I'm, calling someone

I dunno what I'm thinking, doing, but she answers. Gabby

And before she says a word, I just

Everything, all the madness, all the, the

I forward the recording the guy made on my phone

I tell her that I think Rufus is

Rufus is

Oh God I'm gonna cry

I can't focus on what she's saying back

Something about Andrea, she's consulting her teachers, they're asking about David –

I don't care about that!

My body is pulsating with pain, my bones are on fire

Just holding the phone is –

And the skin on the back of my hands, all blotchy

It's my grandad again, his days in the factory, how they'd broken his grip

Now it's happening to me

Back at the lodge

Already midday

Just like he said, the hours snatched away

I'm worried I'm crashing

But I can't, I can't, gotta work out what to do

I have to decide if I can leave or not

And maybe you'll hate this

Cos I know I do –

In any horror

When it's obvious to everyone involved that it's, you know, a fucking horror

You get the fuck out

If Rufus drove down, if his car's nearby –

But I don't have the keys

(I can't actually drive)

Hike to the station, ticket to my mum's…

I was telling David only yesterday about her

If he finds her, if he hunts her down…

I'm gonna pack my bag

*

Your five-minute call

I blink and it's dark and it's time, oh God

David

He sees my phone and my bag and he says

Put those back

And I do. I don't know why I'm

Why I'm standing here, just accepting what's gonna, gonna

He isn't even bothering to smile this time

He knows I know

It's time to do the walk again

It's time to do my job

The Fourth Walk

Tipsy again

Drunk on lack of sleep or fear or what

I'm lurching past the kitchen garden –

Who the fuck has a kitchen garden –

I'm sleepwalking, like a zombie

Like I know I'm dead already

But I have a plan! Half a plan

Before I even reach the woods, fuck the woods

Gonna push through the hedge

Cut across the lawn, push through on the other side, skip the woods entirely –

> *Lights out, lights on.*

The night around me pulses –

> *Lights out, lights on. Jumpscare. (It's here.)*

I'm smashing through twigs and brambles –

> *Lights out, lights on. (It's gone.)*

Hoping that thing can't follow me –

> *Lights out, lights on. Jumpscare. (It's closer.)*

Push push push push push push push –

> *Lights out, lights on. (It's gone.)*

Through the other side! I run across the lawn

The hall is to my left but I'm not gonna look at it

I'm not gonna look at it…

I look at it

I stare at it, I can't help it –

The way it's lit tonight. Like it's charging up

And that is not a normal light –

Windows bleeding eerie green

The ground beneath me ripples

'The very power of the land'

Being drawn to that house, that horror, that –

> *The lights pulse.* JOE *speaks over the thrum:*

A shadow strides towards me!

I think he's gonna – I think he's gonna –

*

Pour me a cup of tea?

Lodge

Not sure how we

David puts the tea in front of me

Drink it

I sip it, staring up at him

It's dark in here, like the night has crept inside

But there's something about the way David stands…

The way he's dressed, been dressed, all this week

The suit

Black and white. Black and white…

Then I realise

The lil waistcoat. The worried face

I've been like this, I've dressed like this

The champagne nights

Handing out fizz

Now I know what he is

Cos he's not the Lord of the manor, he's, he's…

She was right, I say, what Andrea said

The Lindens, are gone

So that must mean –

You're not a Linden

Maybe you, took the name, used the name, tried to be the master

But really, you're a servant

Look at you – you're just a bloody, butler

You're the butler! You're the dogsbody

You think you're fetching the scraps, but you are the scraps –

> JOE *is slapped.*

My grin stays rigid

> JOE *is slapped again.*

He slaps me again and leans in close – his breath like flesh –

I am proud to serve

His eyes are a colour I've never seen before

It's like they're

Yeah, now they're green too

He's gripping my shoulder

Or my neck, can't tell, like he's gonna

Pop some fizz again

But my lips start tingling

Wait, did he kiss me?

I look at the tea. Dirty, and glowing –

Oh fuck

It's drugged

Tea's drugged

Now he's the one grinning

And I'm the one

Gone

And the dreams, no no no no don't let – the dreams –

*

The Third Nightmare

JOE *tumbles into the void.*

It's dizzying, diseased, dirty, decaying...

Friday

Fire, body, wow, mouth, stinging, head, banging, ceiling, staring, move? Nope. No, banging, head, banging? Not head. Not here. Down. Down. Door. Move? Nope. Splinters, shouting, someone, someone's, help. Helpppp

Here. With a stick?

Bat. Baseball bat

Oh my god, Gabby. Gabby! Gabbyyy

> JOE *throws up.*

*

My boss holds my head over the toilet

This is my first time meeting Andrea too, hi

Lil pink-haired geek, horrified by how much I'm

> JOE *throws up again.*

Or maybe it's the way I look

I catch a glimpse of myself in the chrome. Empty. Shrunken

They're sorry they took so long but they needed to prepare

Andrea was finishing her research and got caught up spell checking

Okay? They couldn't find the house

But just before dawn, the dancer found them and showed them the way and –

This is happening too fast

But they have to act fast

Gabby says I need to be taken away, fuck this shit

The grounds of this casa embrujada have poisoned me

But Andrea says they need to tread carefully

She quotes the dancer's story:

'Those unlucky enough to bar Its way were lost to the woods forever'

That's how it got Rufus, he must've got in Its way…

She catches my eye, goes quiet

Gabby wants to know if, I'm okay

And I tell her… I wanna stay, I wanna finish it

Stop this bastard. If he got Rufus, we get him

Andrea pulls out this ancient fuck-off book. Sorry, what's this?

The *Trespass Arcana*

Part walking guide, part curse manual

It has a number of banishment rituals they can try –

Hang on hang on, what did she study again?

She was following David, that's how she met Gabby, she knows this stuff, she

'Spell checking'. I get it

*

The plan is underway. Daphne and Velma are getting into position

Whilst Scooby Doo here is back in his costume, waiting

Staring at the painting

Charles Linden, the sickly boy

They must've propped him up to paint him

Only this time I'm drawn to the background

All painted black

But the closer I look

There's a shape in the black

A shape of a man…

More than a man…

A head…with horns…

But the painted black is all around me now

It's time. I limp to the door

Don't even need him to knock

I throw it open and he's coming down the path

David, looking relieved to see me

He's not surprised mind –

Here is the guy he slapped and drugged

Yet still he's dressed and ready to do his job

Cos that's what my sort do, isn't it?

We get in line, we know our place

That's what David thinks anyway

Money, makes you so sure of everything and everyone

I'm smiling

Giving the performance of my life and I'm smiling

Yeah here we go, motherfucker

Let's walk that final walk…

The Final Walk

…but I'm not, gonna walk

I head to the kitchen garden

This is where I'm to meet him again, the dancer

That's what Gabby said, when they spoke to him before –

And here he is

Keeping to the shadows

A skulled head bowed low

The one who shared his story

Who told me I wasn't alone

Andrea said he offered to take my place

He'll walk the ghost walk one last time, distract that thing for us

Are you sure you wanna do this, that's what I wanna ask him –

But he stares me down with his abandoned eyes

And I can't say anything

Off he goes, towards the hedge, around the house

He knows where he's going

And so do I

*

There's a poem I did in school

And I hated poetry in school

But the title of this one stuck with me

Probably cos it let us swear

'Those Bastards in Their Mansions'

And every time some privileged twat

Has ever crossed my path

I think those words have fluttered inside me, quietly

'Those Bastards in Their Mansions'

They're not so quiet anymore

I'm thinking them over and over, they're getting louder and louder

'Those Bastards in Their Mansions'

As I march up the drive

I think of the rest of them

Those Bastards in Their Mansions, Those Bastards in Their Banks

Those Bastards in Their Penthouses, Their Private Jets, Their Governments –

Right now I could haunt them all

Paragon Hall is dead ahead

David told me to keep away from it and I did, so fucking subservient, so easily told

But not tonight

They join me either side:

Andrea with her book, Gabby with her bat

Closer we get, the hotter the air

Like this house has sucked the heat from the hillside

It has guzzled the warmth and the wealth for too long

At the top of the steps, I see the crack between the doors, ablaze with green

Last chance to turn back

That's never gonna happen

*

Inside the house

Is not a house any more

It's all been, hollowed-out

The wood panels turning back into bark

Shifting, swaying, breathing

And the stink!

Dank and dark and

The sickly green is all around us

The foxfire, the fungus, it's bulging

It's taking us deeper within

Gabby's in front, leading the way

Into this cavern of sweat and rot

A long, earthy tunnel

Brambles like barbed wire

Getting narrower and narrower

I force myself to breathe the stench

Not gonna let it choke me

The roots on the walls, gleaming, writhing as we walk past them –

But they're not roots

Hands

Hands, pushing out!

Dirty, dripping fingers flexing

They snatch at us!

Nails brushing past us, fingertips scuttling across my shirt, in my hair

Getting harder and harder to –

Gabby's slapping the hands away, Andrea's trying to stop her book getting nabbed –

Then something grabs me

It wrenches me up!

But I don't struggle, I don't

Cos as soon as they hold me, there's a, a bolt of understanding –

This is what's left of all those other boys

The ones who walked before me

And what remains of them, they're terrified, of course they are –

But they are on our side

I'm telling them that. I think I'm yelling it

They've got to let us go, they've got to let us –

Go

The squirming stops. All is still

Then a rush of chaos as the hands and arms are yanking and dragging and

They're pushing us through the tiny tunnel

A bright green light. A final roar from the army behind us…

We tumble to the floor

The ground, spongy, greasy, but we made it. They helped us

The tunnel… now empty

Where are we? I think this used to be a ballroom

Furniture spat around the place, half-sunken, half-eaten –

Shriek.

There, at the heart

A sight I will never forget

The mound of foxfire

Tendrils of rotting light

They are wrapped around a shape

That used to be man

Trying still to be a man

Shriek.

The worst thing… somehow… I recognise him

This, is the Lord of the Manor

This is Charles Linden

Sicker than ever

A mouldy jaw hangs loose

Ancestral screams, gurgle out of him

But where the rest of the face should be…

Explodes into a fungal mess, reaching up and up…

It's a really, really, big, head

Shriek.

And there, on his knees

Suckling on a dirty root –

The servant pleasing his master

It's David

He sees us

He's horrified

Shriek.

Andrea starts flicking through the *Trespass Arcana*

Chanting words in a language that shouldn't exist

David leaps up, arms outstretched

But Gabby – striding forth –

Strikes him with her bat, oof

He staggers back but he doesn't fall

The Linden cheers him on

Shriek.

Andrea jumps in to help

David may be strong but he's no match for the pair of them

Especially after a giant hardback to the face, ouch

They force him into a mouldy armchair

Tie him up with vines

I help hold him down

Return the slap from before

Shriek.

Gabby turns back to the master

She's going to take another swing –

But no. She's getting something from the rucksack –

Something that makes my heart swell

It's the blowtorch, from our kitchens

This is for Rufus

Burning, shrieking, chaos…

*

Outside

The three of us watch

The black and white melts to red

Paragon Hall roars with flames

We've laid them all to rest, the master and the servants

We've set the boys free

I turn to Gabby and Andrea

They're holding each other close

I feel like, I should give them a moment? Yeah, I'll

Fetch my stuff from the lodge

It's weird, after the giddy high, now there's just a

Maybe I'll call my mum or

Is there anybody else?

Not really

I suddenly feel, so alone

Except I'm not alone

Something blocks the path

At the edge of the light…

A shadow, with horns

They aren't horns at all, I see that now

They are Its claws, shackled above Its head

I watch the chains snap

As the deal is done. A settled score

It walks around the house no more

Epilogue

> JOE *stands alone.*

You have questions

I'm not giving you answers

Cos the first one you'll ask is, how much of that was true?

And you never ask a storyteller that

If you go to where the hall used to be

You'll find nothing there. Like it never existed

*

I didn't get paid, surprise surprise

And I'm not gonna pretend I fully recovered

Physically, or mentally

But I bounced back. I don't look as rough as before

The skin still sags in places, the hair is turning grey but

That could just be cos I'm working at the bar again

Gabby and Andrea

We're all pretty close now

Andrea's doing a post-doc, still researching weird shit

She started a queer ramblers group actually

Gabby hates it

Loves her new baseball bat though, present from me

She put a plaque in the bar, in the cosiest corner, the snug:

'For Rufus'…

*

I never saw the dancer again

I don't think he told us the truth

Cos it's odd – he said he survived, he helped my friends, he helped me

But when I saw all those boys, in the hall...

I think I felt him in there with them?

Maybe I do believe in ghosts after all

But whether <u>you</u> believe or not...

Not sure a theatre show is gonna be the thing that changes that

I'm just delighted to have staged something, finally

And I wanna thank you all for coming. Just before you go –

In the audience tonight

There's actually a representative of the theatre

The theatre I mentioned them before, the big theatre?

The ones that fucked me over?

Could we get the house lights on please? Just a little bit

The house lights come up.

Don't worry, I'm not gonna point you out

I just want to see who's hiding in this lovely audience. Squirming

Now, this person believes they were invited here by my ex's dad

Because I used his name on the invitation

Funny how that made you come running...

So! The play is over. But there's a twist in the tale

Why do ghosts stick around?

The house lights flicker and dim as JOE *gets out his phone.*

I didn't tell you everything, when I saw It that final night, when I saw It break free

I didn't mean to trick It, catch It… but, turns out
You can trap a monster in a piece of art
Like a portrait in a lodge. Like a picture on a phone
Now I'm the one who has It chained
And I have made another deal
Those Bastards in Our Mansions
Those Bastards in Our Theatres
Everybody keep still please!
Most of you have nothing to fear, but…
It walks around the house tonight

> *The phone camera flashes, plunging the room into darkness.*
> *One final jumpscare – right in the audience.*

*

> *When the horror is over…*
> *Bows to the inappropriate song.*

JURASSIC

'Denying the truth doesn't stop it being true.'

David Attenborough

Jurassic was first performed at Soho Theatre, London, on 18 November 2025. It was produced by Ransack and supported by Arts Council England and ThickSkin Theatre. The cast was as follows:

DEAN	Matt Holt
JAY	Alastair Michael
Playwright	Tim Foley
Director	Piers Black
Assistant Director	Yanni Ng
Set & Costume Designer	Eleanor Ferguson
Movement Director	Yandass Ndlovu
Sound Designer	Anna Short
Sound Design Associate	Patch Middleton
Lighting Designer	Catja Hamilton
Assistant Lighting Designer	Haley Yiu
Senior Producer	ADMA Productions
Creative Producer	Ransack Theatre
Assistant Producer	Louis Lisle
Stage Manager	Olga Morisse
Photography	Tarek Slater
Graphic Design	Madison Coby

Characters

JAY, *an academic*
DEAN, *the dean*

Setting

The Dean's office on a university campus.

Staging

Minimal set.

Notes

(*Beat.*) is short, (*Pause.*) is long, punctuation denotes pacing.

01.

DEAN. Could you clear something up for me?

JAY. Of course

DEAN. Can't remember where I heard it

JAY. Something about me?

DEAN. Something about you. It was a little concerning

JAY. Probably isn't true

DEAN. Is it true you made an appearance on *Countdown*?

JAY. Oh. Ha

DEAN. Is it true

JAY. It is true, yeah

DEAN. And when was that?

JAY. Two, about two years ago, yeah

DEAN. And how did you fare?

JAY (*beat*). Not very well I'm afraid

DEAN. Yes, I heard that too. It's the timer, isn't it. Incredibly stressful

JAY. Ha

DEAN. I just can't watch that show

JAY. It is quite stressful

DEAN. I just can't watch it. I'm weirdly, squeamish about that kind thing; watching, people, flounder

JAY (*beat*). I didn't flounder

DEAN. They should consider getting rid of it

JAY. I did quite well in some rounds

DEAN. And people would do a lot better, wouldn't they?

JAY. Sorry, getting rid of

DEAN. The timer

JAY. Oh. Ha

DEAN. Yes? You agree?

JAY. Yes. Well, no, they can't do that

DEAN. Why not?

JAY. It's, *Countdown*. Something has to, count down. (*Beat*.) I wasn't playing to win. That's clear if you see the episode. You win a teapot. I don't even drink tea, so

DEAN. You were playing for second place

JAY. Yeah. Suppose

DEAN. And what do you win for second place?

JAY (*beat*). Was this the reason you asked to....?

DEAN. No no, we haven't properly been introduced, have we. I'm the new Dean. Dean

JAY. Yes, Dean the new Dean, everybody's delighted about that

DEAN. Delighted about what

JAY. Your, arrival, very nice to meet you

DEAN. Yes. I haven't met all the teaching staff yet, there's something of a, transition at the moment

JAY. I've noticed

DEAN. You'll be aware of how it was before

JAY. Yeah, it was getting a little…

DEAN. A little what

JAY. What were you going to say?

DEAN. Overstaffed

JAY. Yep

DEAN. But now it will be different

JAY. Looking forward to it

DEAN. Change is, important

JAY. Absolutely

DEAN. I'm glad you understand

JAY. And if you need help getting to know the department…

DEAN. Thank you, I'm, getting to know it

JAY. But hopefully there's a chance I'll be working with you, in a, a larger capacity, soon, possibly. (*Beat.*) My application

DEAN. Oh

JAY. Forrrr

DEAN. Department Head, yes

JAY. Yeah, well. With Sandra leaving and, uh, most of the senior staff being told to move on as well –

DEAN. They weren't told that

JAY. No

DEAN. They simply had things explained to them

JAY. Yep

DEAN. The new set of circumstances. The times they are a-changing

JAY. Dylan

DEAN. No no. Dean

JAY (*beat*). Right. Well I don't mean to be, presumptuous. But it's got to be someone. Department Head. And there aren't that many of us left! I know my inexperience might count against me, but I thought I'd, you know. Throw my hat into the ring

DEAN. What hat

JAY (*beat*). Any hat

DEAN. Jay – may I call you Jay?

JAY. Of course, 'Dean'

DEAN. There is something much more important we need to discuss

JAY. Absolutely

DEAN. And you know what this is about

JAY. I don't think so?

DEAN. You don't?

JAY. Unless this is. The student bars thing?

DEAN. What about the student bars?

JAY. Then it isn't, about that? Which is nothing

DEAN. Well this isn't nothing. I can't believe you're not aware of the news

JAY. What news?

DEAN. Perhaps you haven't processed it. In some ways it's bad news, terrible news for you

JAY (*beat*). S'fine, who got it?

DEAN. Jay

JAY. I knew it was a long shot, but. An interview at least

DEAN. Nobody got Department Head

JAY (*beat*). Is Sandra staying on? She wouldn't. She was bitching and moaning about everything that's. About you, specifically. You don't want Sandra, she keeps a hip flask in her office – in a nook, behind a painting, of an ammonite – no, she's making jibes about me going to the student bars, but there's no actual rule against that, and there is an actual rule about alcohol, in your office, in case that, changes anything

DEAN. Everything is changing! We have to completely reformat. I say 'bad news', but you must recognise that it's good news, Jay, extraordinary news

JAY. You're losing me

DEAN. Yes. (*Beat.*) We're losing the entire department

JAY. What. The entire

DEAN. All of Palaeontology. Can't be helped

JAY. No but I was, reassured, barely what, three months ago –

DEAN. Before my time –

JAY. Our funding is ring-fenced –

DEAN. Nothing to do with funding. Or fencing. Or rings. There has been a tremendous advancement in science, Jay. They have recently developed… a new technology. I'm amazed you haven't heard! This is big, Jay. Bigger than big. Giant. Gigantic. Jurassic!

JAY. What's going on

DEAN. They've gone and brought them back, Jay. They've brought the dinosaurs back

JAY (*beat*).

DEAN. On an island. One hundred and twenty miles west of Costa Rica. I don't fully understand the process, it was only announced last night. They extract the DNA from samples of dinosaur blood, found inside mosquitoes, preserved in amber. They then construct clones, Jay, clones from prehistoric blueprints. You have to see it to believe it! Herds of diplodocuses! Swarms of velociraptors! And even – if you can fathom it – a Tyrannosaurus Rex

JAY. And are they all kept… in a park?

DEAN. Why yes! In a Jurassic park! I've been looking online, refreshing the news, waiting all morning to be emailed a, press release, nothing as of yet, Jay, but it's coming. The future, is coming

JAY. And in this park. There's an old guy, yeah? White beard, walking stick, questionable Scottish accent –

DEAN. So you know him

JAY. Couple of kids too? And a man called Sam Neill

DEAN. I was paying more attention to the dinosaurs, if I'm honest. Sam Neill, is he the project leader?

JAY. This is a joke

DEAN. No joke

JAY (*beat*). *Jurassic Park*

DEAN. Yes

JAY. No it's, *Jurassic Park*. It's a film

DEAN. They filmed it, yes

JAY. No I mean it's, made-up. It's not real. It's a story

DEAN. I don't understand

JAY. A story, a film. This has to be a bit

DEAN. A bit of what

JAY. You aren't actually gonna fire me because you watched *Jurassic Park*

DEAN. Don't think I made the choice lightly. But I was brought into this university because the Principal wants me to make difficult decisions, wherever possible. And this is one of them. Think about it, Jay, there won't be a need for palaeontologists. If we can study these creatures, these dinosaurs, in reality…

JAY. This is not reality

DEAN. Jay, Jay. Happens all the time in academia, disciplines fall away, the world moves on –

JAY. It's a film, Dean. How many times do I – it's not even a recent film, it's from like, the early nineties –

DEAN. I can't be expected to know when they started the research –

JAY. They haven't started anything! It's a film, it's a fake

DEAN. I saw this with my own eyes, Jay

JAY. What you saw, wasn't real. It was a film. About a fictional event. In a fictional place. With fictional, science, science, <u>fiction</u>, can't be done. Dinosaurs, can't be cloned from, prehistoric insects and they definitely can't be roaming the Earth today, they just. Can't

DEAN (*beat*). I don't want a staff member who says Can't, Jay

JAY. Oh come on

DEAN. I'll need you to clear your desk by the end of the day

JAY. This is. Fuck!

DEAN. I'm heading to a meeting, by the time I'm back I expect you to have vacated the premises –

JAY. I have lectures! I have students!

DEAN. Not any more and, not any more. Please don't make me call security

JAY. We don't have security! I wanna speak to the principal about this

DEAN. She's away on a fundraising trip, she won't want disturbing

JAY. To the, the chancellor then –

DEAN. He's finishing his term at the end of next month, he doesn't want a fuss

JAY. This is my, career, Dean, you can't go pissing it away because you're, look – okay – if we both just take a moment –

DEAN. I don't need a moment

JAY. Then you, are a fucking idiot. And you haven't heard the last of this

02.

DEAN. Jay

JAY. 'Dean'

DEAN. Good of you to come in. I'd offer you a chair, but we sold a lot of the furniture

JAY. So is everyone just gonna, stand

DEAN. That's the spirit

JAY. Gotta tighten that belt

DEAN. What belt

JAY. Any belt

DEAN. We'll buy back the chairs when we're a little more solvent. The university is under a tremendous deal of pressure financially, and I feel that pressure on me – so if I previously behaved, a little erratically…

JAY. Uh-huh

DEAN. I'm just trying to give you the context for last month's, discussion

JAY. Is this a build-up to an apology?

DEAN. There will be an apology, if you're patient

JAY. I have been out of work for the last month, I haven't even had my last paycheque –

DEAN. You need to speak to the Finance Department about that –

JAY. I'm speaking to anyone who'll listen

DEAN. Because there are other monetary matters to sort out as well. You'll be docked for a cleaning bill, of course, you left a box of stuff in your office

JAY. I see. We're being petty

DEAN. You're the petty one, Jay. It struck me as an act of defiance

JAY. Consider it a donation. And you know what – you can use the box as a stool. Let's skip ahead to the apology

DEAN. Let me find my statement

JAY. Don't want a statement, I want an apology. Your apology

DEAN (*beat*). I suppose I remember most of it. (*Beat.*) When we spoke together on the morning of. See, I can't recall the date

JAY. I'm not bothered about the date –

DEAN. I'm bothered about the date! That's why I prepared a statement, I'm trying to be accurate

JAY. So now you want to be accurate

DEAN. When we spoke together, on the morning of, whenever it was, I was tired and, yes, perhaps a little confused

JAY. So is this you admitting…

DEAN. I now acknowledge, that *Jurassic Park*, is not real. It is a film

JAY (*beat*). Thank you

DEAN. In my defence. It is not just a film. It is a film, franchise

JAY. How is that a defence?

DEAN. I'm saying there's more than one film. In fact, there's quite a number of them. We've been, bombarded, as a society, with clips of dinosaurs, tropical islands, middle-aged men in shorts

JAY. Okay

DEAN. Is it any wonder, some would think, it's reality?

JAY. Nobody thinks it's reality

DEAN. Ah-ah. You can't make unverified statements like that. Especially since we know it isn't true. I was deceived, however briefly. If I was, others were too

JAY. Yes keep, telling yourself that

DEAN. Sheer exposure! Information overload! We'll reach a point when there are more *Jurassic* films than, pages on the internet

JAY. Okay. Talking of unverified statements –

DEAN. Not a statement. It's a matter of opinion. And, speaking as a victim, my opinion is more qualified than most

JAY. You're the victim? I'm the victim! Wrongful dismissal! I've been, physically sick, mentally stressed, I did a good job till all this, a really good job, this is not how I should be treated

DEAN. And for that, I can apologise

JAY. Yes you can

DEAN. There we go. (*Pause.*) Thanks for coming in

JAY. Hang on. Is that it?

DEAN. Do you want me to repeat the apology

JAY. There's, the small matter of, my reinstatement?

DEAN. Oh

JAY. Yes

DEAN. You want your job back?

JAY. Yes

DEAN. That was a, query, not an offer. You're not getting your job back

JAY. I'm sorry?

DEAN. Is that your apology?

JAY. My?

DEAN. I apologise, you apologise

JAY. What am I apologising for?

DEAN. We saw what you did. We all did, the whole faculty. Even, and I hate to mention it, the Principal. She saw what you did too

JAY. What did I do?

DEAN. You took to social media. That very evening. I have the dates for that too, written down, you publicly complained

JAY. Of course I did!

DEAN. 'Speaking to anyone who'll listen.' Your own words

JAY. Yeah, so?

DEAN. And the complaints kept coming, didn't they? Days and days of damning commentary. Getting others involved, trying to whip up momentum. You gave all sorts of interviews to the student radio. They wrote all sorts of articles in the student press. We were asked for comments, statements, hounded for days

JAY. Good

DEAN. Not good, Jay. You brought the department into disrepute. The entire university!

JAY. Well, rightly so

DEAN. Why rightly so? Because your new Dean is a fucking idiot?

JAY. You said it

DEAN. No. You said it. Your own words, again. That was your parting remark, the last time we spoke. In this very office

JAY. And was I wrong?

DEAN. You were indeed. Because I'm not an idiot. Yes, I was briefly duped into, accepting a Steven Spielberg film as truth. That's the name of the director

JAY. I've heard of Steven Spielberg

DEAN. Then it may interest you to learn he's made films based on real events before. *Schindler's List. Jaws.* So, following my assertion, listening to your rebuttal, I did some research. I realised my mistake. I learnt the truth. Therefore, to continue to think of me, as an idiot, nay, as a fucking idiot, would ignore the important fact that I am able to learn the truth

JAY (*beat*). No you're still a fucking idiot

DEAN. I have two degrees, Jay. I have a long, long history of university management. You can't tell me that all the faculties I've been associated with – studied for, worked at, hired by – they don't all think I'm an idiot. Unless they themselves are idiots

JAY (*beat*).

DEAN. And if you <u>are</u> insinuating they're idiots, then, like I said, you bring the department into disrepute, the entire university into disrepute, but worse, worse than that, Jay – you bring me, into disrepute. And any individual who is a part of a system, is the system, so this university is clearly a system you cannot be a part of. Ergo, we cannot take you back. QED. That's Latin, Jay

JAY (*beat*). I wanna speak to the Principal

DEAN. Principal agrees with me

JAY. No

DEAN. And she is on a fundraising trip, so

JAY. Same one? Another one? She'll want to speak to me. Cos I'll speak up again

DEAN. Oh yes, to all your followers. You've had quite the popularity spike in recent weeks. That's not to say you were completely unknown beforehand, I'm sure you gained some attention after that disastrous *Countdown* appearance –

JAY. Alright, let's not go there –

DEAN. Another thing that brought the university into disrepute, lest we forget –

JAY. It was one bad numbers round

DEAN. But despite your repeated attempts at sabotage – the university survived

JAY. I'm not trying to destroy the place! I care about this institution. I've worked here longer than you

DEAN. But I'm here for the long run. You fail to get your promotion, you stomp off in a sulk, make as much noise as possible

JAY. That's not what happened at all! I didn't go quietly, yes, only to call out the, the absurdity of this. The absurdity of you. And if you think things are going to die down –

DEAN. They already have

JAY. I will continue to kick up a fuss

DEAN. I've no doubt you'll try. But now that I've apologised… I expect your campaign's been somewhat depleted

JAY. Then I'll find another, 'campaign'. (*Beat.*) The Chancellor's stepping down soon

DEAN. What about it?

JAY. And the student body, they'll be choosing a new one. An election. A campaign. It would give the winner, a platform. (*Beat.*) When do nominations have to –

DEAN. I'm sure the deadline's passed –

JAY. I'm sure it hasn't

DEAN. Jay

JAY. Ahhh. (*Sing-song.*) I think I found my new campaaaaign!

DEAN. Please think very carefully about what you're proposing

JAY. Are you going to give me back my job?

DEAN. That's just not possible

JAY. Are you gonna, say, double my severance pay?

DEAN. That's just not possible either

JAY. Well then. Do excuse me, Dean. I need to head to some student bars. Oh, and. One more thing. (*Beat.*) You're still a fucking idiot

03.

DEAN. Jay

JAY. Dean. My campaign manager thinks I shouldn't be talking to you

DEAN. Indeed?

JAY. The opposition

DEAN. I'm impartial

JAY. Course you are

DEAN. And who is your current campaign manager, Claudia Armitage?

JAY. I see what you're doing

DEAN. What am I doing?

JAY. What you said

DEAN. What did I say?

JAY. 'Current'

DEAN. I'm merely noting how you kept changing the student signatory on your nomination forms

JAY. Yes I did originally have two third years running my campaign

DEAN. And what happened to them?

JAY. You know full well

DEAN. Thought I was an idiot. Idiots don't know anything

JAY. Both of them – Kate Andrews, Charlotte Baker – both of them extremely experienced at running student campaigns. Both of them mysteriously unmatriculated

DEAN. Mysteriously what?

JAY. Unmatriculated

DEAN. No, sorry?

JAY. They were matriculated at the beginning of their studies, and now they are not

DEAN. But I don't think 'unmatriculated' is a word

JAY. Unmatriculated, dematriculated –

DEAN. I don't think either of those are words. So maybe they were never matriculated to begin with

JAY. But they were

DEAN. Yet since one can't be 'unmatriculated', or 'dematriculated', maybe they weren't

JAY. They're third years! Do you know what that means? It means, they've been here, for three years! They can't randomly be, whatever you call it, 'dis-enrolled' in their third year, I don't care if there aren't any words for it!

DEAN. But you should! You can't go around making up technical terms, Jay. This isn't Palaeontology

JAY (*beat*).

DEAN. Look, Admissions and Enrolment is a complex department. I'm just a fucking idiot so maybe I don't understand it, but it sounds like you don't either

JAY. I understand perfectly. But it hasn't stopped me from running

DEAN. Yes, you found an impressionable fresher –

JAY. Claudia is not impressionable –

DEAN. And her mother is a wealthy donor to the university –

JAY. So her matriculation can't be called into question, mmmm. That's not the reason I picked her. But I won't deny, it's helpful

DEAN. Mrs Armitage will not want her daughter corrupted

JAY. I'm not corrupting her

DEAN. Distracted then. It's a real shame when first years prioritise, extracurricular activities

JAY. University politics is an admirable cause

DEAN. I'm sure it is. To some. But maybe we should keep an eye on Claudia

JAY. You're planning to spy on my allies

DEAN. Your 'allies'? We're not at war! 'Allies'! Honestly, making up words, misappropriating others… All I'm saying is, we may offer Claudia some Student Support. Monitor her progress

JAY. Student Support

DEAN. Student Support

JAY. Student Surveillance

DEAN. It's not surveillance! We have better things to do than watch Claudia Armitage and three of her friends enter the Central Library at 3.22 p.m. this afternoon to put up six A3 posters on the central notice board

JAY. So you *are* spying on us!

DEAN. The posters were removed, of course, your team failed to register the correct permit

JAY. Your tactics, in this race, are abominable. But I'm gonna rise above it. I've spoken to the students. This university is going to shit, you know? It's broke, it is broken. Even you have to admit that, every time I come in here it looks as though the place has been ransacked

DEAN. I am clearing all educational environments of unnecessary clutter –

JAY. The students want investment

DEAN. It's not about what they want…

JAY. Housing, better facilities, better services –

DEAN. …it's about what they need

JAY. Yes. And they need me. I wondered if I was being, petty, like you said, running for this position, but I've come to realise that I can actually do some good as Chancellor. And when I win – and I will win –

DEAN. You will not win

JAY. Ohhh, you're gonna make sure of that? Is this why you asked me here, to threaten me?

DEAN. I'm simply saying, you won't win. You shouldn't be running in the first place, Jay; you are predisposed to losing

JAY. What the hell does that mean?

DEAN. When I heard you lost on *Countdown* –

JAY. Oh come on!

DEAN. When you confirmed for me the rumours that you had disgraced yourself on national television. I knew then, at that moment, you were going to lose your job. Because then it was meant to be

JAY. It wasn't 'meant to be'. You fired me

DEAN. I can't be held accountable for something that was always going to happen. I was the cause, yes. But the effect, would always be the same

JAY. You wanna know why I lost on *Countdown*? (*Beat.*) Doesn't matter. Make something up, invent your own sordid narrative

DEAN. 'Invent', from the Latin '*invenere*'; 'to discover'. When one invents something, one discovers something. And I've discovered something else, Jay. You see this, is why I asked you here. It wasn't to bicker. It was to present you, with the facts

JAY. And what are the facts

DEAN. *Jurassic Park* was released in 1993

JAY (*sighs*).

DEAN. The cast included Sam Neill, Laura Dern, Jeff Goldblum… and Richard Attenborough. Do you know who Richard Attenborough's brother is, Jay?

JAY. Yep

DEAN. Who

JAY. Is this – David Attenborough

DEAN. David Attenborough, the renowned natural historian and public broadcaster. And do you know what David Attenborough was doing in the year 2000?

JAY (*beat*). Not off the top of my head

DEAN. He made a documentary called *Living with Dinosaurs*. Funny that

JAY. What

DEAN. His brother, Richard, in a film about dinosaurs… two of them in fact, he was briefly in the 1997 sequel, *The Lost World*…

JAY. Terrible film

DEAN. And here is David, a mere three years later, making his own film about those creatures

JAY (*beat*). So?

DEAN. So the facts speak for themselves

JAY. The facts aren't speaking, they're rambling incoherently

DEAN. I haven't finished. Do you know who was one of the advisers on this documentary, *Living with Dinosaurs*?

JAY. Nope

DEAN. Dr Philip Parry. And do you know who Dr Philip Parry is, Jay?

JAY. Uh, yes. My old tutor

DEAN. You really expect me to believe this is all a coincidence?

JAY (*beat*). I have no fucking clue what you're on about

DEAN. Years in the making! Can't have been easy. I'll admit, it was neat, an impressive feat, the man you call Sam Neill was particularly convincing

JAY. Are you saying I helped make *Jurassic Park*?

DEAN. I'm saying you were complicit

JAY. Do you know how old I was in 1993?

DEAN. We've already acknowledged, with little Claudia, the young can be corrupted

JAY. I remember wanting the fucking, dinosaur lunch box, but I honestly can't – you're going back on yourself now cos you admitted, you fully admitted, that *Jurassic Park* is just a film

DEAN. It unequivocally is a film, yes

JAY. Right

DEAN. But not just a film

JAY. A film franchise, yep

DEAN. It's even more than that now. It is no less than political propaganda, Jay! Designed to be so realistic, so that educated people, highly-educated like myself, would be tricked into believing it was real. And then, we'd be embarrassed, compromised. Our word couldn't be trusted. The system would fall. Throughout the university – mayhem!

JAY. It's already a madhouse

DEAN. I've watched the whole film now, something I couldn't stomach before, have you studied it recently? At the very start there are less than fifty seconds of credits. Only three lines of text:

'Universal Pictures Presents'

'An Amblin Entertainment Production'

'*Jurassic Park*'

…that's it

JAY. This is madness

DEAN. Is it any wonder I missed them? Almost as though they're designed to be missed. No names of actors, directors, nothing like that, no, the full credits are at the end of the film. When everybody has stopped watching

JAY. That's just what films do, put credits at the end

DEAN. And why at the end? They're lying to you for as long as possible!

JAY. I can't, do this, you're going off on one again, you need to take your crazy pills or something

DEAN. Stop doing that. Stop implying I'm of reduced mental capacity, 'madhouse', 'this is madness', you're trying to suggest my points aren't valid

JAY. Well your points aren't valid

DEAN. Does that make me unwell? A little academic respect, for a differing opinion, that's all this conversation warrants

JAY. I have no respect for this

DEAN. I can see that. Just answer me one question, Jay. What's your background? Your parents, are they university educated?

JAY. That's two questions

DEAN. Your, comfort. Your cockiness. You're how old and you assumed you'd be considered for Department Head? Look at you now, running to be Chancellor! You've been coddled, coaxed, but you haven't been, challenged. And when you are, you lose. That's a symptom of a liberal upbringing

JAY. Oh right, so you have me all pegged yeah? Left-leaning household. Read the *Guardian*, did recycling

DEAN. I didn't say left-leaning, I said liberal

JAY. Oh pardon me

DEAN. No this is interesting. What do you think liberal means?

JAY. Maybe you could give me the Latin etymology

DEAN. So you don't have a definition

JAY. Liberal. 'Believes in liberty'

DEAN. Is that it

JAY. 'Open to new ideas'. 'Humanistic'

DEAN. So if you're having some toast and being liberal with the butter are you being humanistic?

JAY. You're using the word in a different context

DEAN. Ah, you only want the context to suit you. Classic liberal

JAY. That's not how I was raised, actually. No *Guardian*, no recycling. You got that wrong, Dean

DEAN. You're the one who set the parameters, not me

JAY. But I haven't been 'coddled', I haven't been 'coaxed'. Want the checklist? State-school education. Single-parent household. You know what, we <u>did</u> do a lot of recycling, the number of bottles my mum got through. Our bit for the planet. David Attenborough would be pleased. How about you?

DEAN. I have no opinion on your recycling

JAY. No, how about you, what's your background, if I'm giving you mine

DEAN. I already said. Two degrees. A long, long history of university management –

JAY. Family. If you have one. Cos I'll tell you the 'symptom', of mine, yeah? I am cocky. Not a genius. Still got beaten by a sweet old lady on *Countdown*. But I am clever. And I fight. I succeed against the odds

DEAN. But I succeed against the odds

JAY. What odds? You're stacking them against me, you're in a position of power

DEAN. You are in a position of power too

JAY. How the fuck am I?

DEAN. You are the façade, the Amblin Entertainment Production, the relentless conspiracy of reptilian lies since the early 1990s

JAY. <u>It was a film</u>

DEAN. We'll see if others agree with you. Because I am going to announce it

JAY. Announce what

DEAN. I'll make a brief statement about the Attenboroughs

JAY. Saying what

DEAN. Outlining your plan to destroy this institution! We'll release it via student media

JAY. You're seriously going public with your insane – ha! Yeah, fine, great, go ahead

DEAN. I will

JAY. Press release, something, whatever, shout it from the roof of the campus!

DEAN. When this is all made public, there'll have to be an investigation. And during that time, we'll have to suspend your election budget

JAY. Fine, why don't we. (*Beat.*) Oh. Ohhh, I see what you're up to. Then there's method in the madness

DEAN. Stop it

JAY. And how long will this investigation take? Until polling day?

DEAN. It's possible it will take until then, yes

JAY. You're scared, aren't you? Who's the Principal backing again?

DEAN. She's not backing anyone

JAY. Lord Richard Owen. Some ancient Tory minister! Have you seen his voting record? You really think students are going to pick him over me? Claudia is designing a beautiful leaflet. It's got a list of Owen's political views on one side, our slogan on the other: We Don't Want Any Dinosaurs. Geddit?

DEAN. I do, indeed, get it. But if you're forbidden to utilise any campaign finances, how are you going to print these leaflets?

JAY (*beat*). We'll make it an e-leaflet

DEAN. Oh, an 'e-leaflet', Lord Owen will be terrified

JAY. We're still gonna beat him. He's never even visited the campus! I live this place. I breathe this place. I was so upset when you tried to take it away from me, this is not the path I wanted my career to take, but I realise now, it's a necessary one. I am gonna win this, Dean. Gonna win this fair and square

04.

JAY. You cheating bastard

DEAN. Jay

JAY. You lying, fucking snake

DEAN. You can't lay the blame on me

JAY. Course I fucking can

DEAN. The people have spoken

JAY. I'm gonna appeal. There is no precedent, for a last-minute substitution of a candidacy –

DEAN. I'm afraid there is. Back in 1981, there was a similar situation. One of the nominees had to step back from the campaign for health reasons, just like Lord Owen

JAY. All very convenient

DEAN. Not for his Lordship. A problem with his heart medication, so I'm told

JAY. Yeah, whatever, hope he recovers. Slowly

DEAN. Now now, Jay. Nobody likes a sore loser

JAY. But I wouldn't have lost against him!

DEAN. People vote for a name they recognise. I know you had your, online presence, your e-leaflets, but in the end it wasn't enough. The students have found a real celebrity

JAY. Of all the possible replacements, why did you have to pick him?

DEAN. I don't know what you mean

JAY. Why did you have to pick him! Sam Fucking Neill!

DEAN. We're delighted he accepted the candidacy. Sometimes these celebrities don't want anything to do with universities, even honorary positions, but we rang him up and he agreed to take on the role. A sensible man. Clear-eyed about the future. You know I believe he's excited about some of the challenges ahead

JAY. I hate Sam Neill

DEAN. I'd say he hates you too, but he has no idea who you are. Though he owes you a great deal. Your slogan really worked, We Don't Want Any Dinosaurs, well, yes, Sam Neill was the perfect candidate for that, wasn't he?

JAY. I want to speak to him

DEAN. Sam's a busy man

JAY. He has to understand why I was doing this – the whole point of my protest –

04.   99

DEAN. The Principal's explained everything to him about the position. And Sam's flying out to join her on her next fundraising trip, so that's excellent news for the Finance Department

JAY. This is a stitch-up!

DEAN. No. This was good organisation. There were no dirty tricks, no propaganda films, no brotherly pacts –

JAY. Just the removal of our election budget and a completely ludicrous smear campaign

DEAN. Ah, yes, so you saw my statement? About the devious Attenboroughs?

JAY. Absolute fucking nonsense

DEAN. Attenborough has been trending all day! We've been getting hits as far away as Russia. But how was your statement? Your, concession speech? I know they've been live-streaming the results. Couldn't bring myself to watch it, you know how I feel about people floundering. Perhaps I'll permit an exception. Yes, I'll find the recording. And make a little toast. To a worthy victory

JAY. You can take your little toast and shove it up. (*Beat.*) I'll report you

DEAN. For what

JAY. Not about the election. Not even about the Attenborough stuff. You've got alcohol, on the premises

DEAN. What alcohol?

JAY. Any alcohol. I'm pretty sure that's against university regulations. In fact I'm very sure

DEAN. There is no alcohol

JAY *pulls out a hip flask.*

JAY. Here we are. Yes, I just found this hip flask in your desk

DEAN. No you didn't

JAY. And it's funny… it looks exactly like the one I was about to retrieve. In a nook, behind a painting, of an ammonite. Helping yourself to Sandra's old supplies, were you?

DEAN. No I wasn't

JAY. Come on, Dean. I've seen you drink from it. And others have too

DEAN. No they haven't

JAY. I'll talk to some of my 'allies'… Yes, and they'll recall what they've seen…

DEAN. Jay. Jay

JAY. One ex-student, yeah, it's coming back to me now. Kate Andrews, she told me you had alcohol on your breath. And another, Charlotte Baker, she said you were behaving erratically. A distinct slurring in your voice

DEAN. Retract that at once

JAY. Looking back, it would explain why you mistook a Hollywood blockbuster for real life

DEAN. No I didn't

JAY. Just some late-night repeat. You started watching it few drinks in, you were tired, you were emotional, you were – oh, you were lonely. Cos there's nobody else at home, is there? No Mrs Dean. No Mr Dean. No Little Deans running around the place. It's why you care so much about your stupid job. Cos your life is shit and you've nothing else to live for. And it's all gone wrong. I'm not the only one who's made a name for myself, am I. Dean the Dean, the stupid joke, the fucking nutter who sold the chairs. The Blessed Principal will know this, even if she's never here. She's probably planning to get rid of you. Maybe all she needs is an excuse

DEAN. There's no basis to these allegations

JAY. There is when I make them. Cos I know the signs, see. My mum, the drinking. That's how I lost her

DEAN. Another thing you've lost

JAY (*beat. Chuckle. Beat*). *Countdown*. Was her favourite show. That's the only reason I went on. And a week before my episode recorded, a week… she got sick, she died. So yes, maybe my head wasn't in the game, to win. But this is what you don't get, Dean. I don't just lose. I lose and keep going

DEAN. Jay. Wait

JAY. Nope, gotta go. Things to do. To destroy you. We'll be overturning the vote. If you think everyone's a fan of Sam Neill, you're very much mistaken. Even tonight, there are protests planned. Goodbye, Dean. Oh! I just thought. When you lose this job. You're gonna have to change your name

JAY *exits.*

DEAN. No! I, am Dean. I, am, Dean!

05.

JAY. I came as requested. Not to gloat. Not entirely

DEAN. Jay

JAY. Certainly getting a little wild out there

DEAN. A petty distraction

JAY. You didn't think the protests would last this long, did you? Good job you sold the furniture, they'd be putting it through the windows

DEAN. Retract the allegations you made against me

JAY. Can't do that

DEAN. Can't, or won't?

JAY. Can't and won't, sorry

DEAN. You're not sorry

JAY. You're right I'm not

DEAN. You say things and you never mean them. Lies upon lies, Jay, that's always been your problem. The world is sickened by it. Rotting away

JAY. Is somebody feeling the heat? I could tell you the average temperature of the Earth during the Jurassic period, if that helps

DEAN. I'm feeling cool and collected. I'm simply making a request

JAY. And I can't fulfil that request. Ah! 'Won't'

DEAN. This is, a negotiation, Jay. This is why you're here. I'm authorised to make you an offer. We can finally give you your severance pay

JAY. I'm not interested

DEAN. Half of what you requested

JAY. I'm still not. (*Beat.*) Do you mean double?

DEAN. No, half

JAY. That's shit negotiation

DEAN. Do you know what I had to do, to get this offer? I had to fly out to meet the Principal. I had to pay, personally, for my own plane ticket, meet her between meetings to beg her. Beg her, Jay

JAY. All for nothing then

DEAN. I don't think so. Because she has agreed that if the allegations are dropped, if you take this severance sum, if you sign a non-disclosure agreement, if the anarchy on campus is ended… I can keep my job

JAY. No biggie

DEAN. So you agree to my terms?

JAY. You're not listening. And you never listen. Can you hear the students? It's not about dinosaurs any more, it's not even about Sam Neill. It's something else now. Something bigger. A fundamental rage at the way things are run. Those students camped outside your office – they won't move on. Not until you do

DEAN. I will deal with them later. For now, I deal with you. You've applied for other jobs. Oh, yes, maybe I've been spying on you after all. Or maybe, your prospective employers have asked me for a reference. I'm the fucking idiot, but you're the one putting me as a referee, riddle me that!

JAY. Of course I didn't put you down, they'll have gone through the system

DEAN. Now you get it! People always want to go through the system! Because they themselves are the system. The system of hiring, the system of campaigning, the system of protest! And now, the system of cooperation

JAY. Well the system is broken

DEAN. No it isn't

JAY. Yes it is

DEAN. No it isn't

JAY. Yes it is! Give me one good reason to work with you

DEAN. It would require you to take a leap of imagination

JAY. I'm leaping

DEAN. Marjory Litherland

JAY (*beat*). Who?

DEAN. The name means nothing to you?

JAY. No. (*Beat.*) Um. Wasn't she…

DEAN. The one…

JAY. Who…

DEAN. Beat you on *Countdown*? Yes, she was

JAY. Oh. (*Beat.*) Why bring her up

DEAN. I just wondered if, you remembered her

JAY. Of course I remember her, what about her?

DEAN. I was imagining she was dead, poor thing

JAY. Why?

DEAN. Oh you know

JAY. No? She's not dead. I mean, not as far as I'm aware, why would you imagine that?

DEAN. She was only in her sixties

JAY. Okay?

DEAN. And that's no age to go, is it

JAY. No? (*Beat.*) Yeah no I don't get what you're saying

DEAN. I tracked her down. Social media. It says you're friends on there. 'Friends', you couldn't even remember who she was!

JAY. Why did you track her down?

DEAN. I wanted to see who beat you. See what we had in common. And then I let my imagination run away with me, as one tends to do when one scrolls through all those posts and pictures. I wondered if she was happy. I wondered if she was dead. And if she were dead, I imagine the death might not be treated as suspicious. Not initially

JAY. But she's not, dead

DEAN. Who's to say she wasn't on, I don't know, medication? People on medication don't seem to fare very well around here. Think of Lord Owen. So, if Marjory had died, the police might receive an anonymous tip-off about her death. They might discover something sordid, something very sordid indeed

JAY (*beat*). But she's not dead

DEAN. Imagine that she is. Imagine that somebody visited her address, Marjory had a habit of inviting people in, if they looked like the right sort of people. And liberal academics tend to look like the right sort of people. They're dangerous like that, very dangerous indeed

JAY. Dean. What are you saying

DEAN. The police would discover that this visitor, after doctoring Marjory's pills, left something behind. People leave stuff behind all the time. You left a box of items in your office, didn't you? That was a silly thing to do. What if somebody got their hands on it? What if somebody rifled through your personal effects and planted, let's think, a dropped glove of yours at the scene of the crime? But that's terribly gauche. Maybe they'd leave, a book about dinosaurs, ah, no, too obvious. You know what I'd do? (*Beat.*) I'd extract your DNA from a follicle of hair that I found on a brush. I'd wipe it round the rim of a mug. And to top it all off, the finishing touch: Marjory's *Countdown* teapot, smashed upon the kitchen floor. You'd like to believe the police could put two and two together – something you could barely do on the numbers round – and they'd come to the imaginative conclusion that her old rival, fired academic, failed campaigner, aggressive protester, was somehow involved

JAY. Are you saying

DEAN. I'm not saying anything

JAY. But are you actually saying

DEAN. I'm merely imagining

JAY. You imagine this happened

DEAN. For a fucking idiot, I have a great deal of imagination

JAY. This is, no. Nope. No, it's impossible

DEAN. No it isn't

JAY (*beat*). Oh my God. Marjory? But she was just a, a sweet old lady

DEAN. No she wasn't. She humiliated you! And considering your mother had died only four days earlier, well. Maybe that's how you justified it

JAY. What

DEAN. Revenge

JAY. No. No no no

DEAN. It's an excellent motive

JAY. But my mum didn't – that's not when she died

DEAN. Pardon?

JAY. She didn't die, before I went on *Countdown*. She died like, a year later

DEAN. You stated otherwise

JAY. Got the date wrong

DEAN (*beat*). You really are bad at numbers

JAY. Right, yeah, fine, made up a fucking sob story to fucking shut you up! I didn't think you'd, fuck

DEAN. No matter. Then Marjory's murder was politically motivated. It was all there in her social media – bitter, Brexit, flags out the window. Everything a liberal like you detests, really, yes, that's why you killed her

JAY. I didn't do anything! I didn't. When did it happen?

DEAN. Wednesday night. Between the hours of 8 and 10 p.m. And I imagine you won't account for your movements

JAY. But I can, I can account!

DEAN. I said won't, not can't. I know you can tell me where you were; you were having sex with Claudia Armitage. (*Beat.*) Yes we were spying on you that time. We've implemented all sorts of new surveillance measures because of these protests. We do know what's been going on between you two

JAY. It was just – the one time –

DEAN. No it wasn't. Remember, you have quite the reputation, Jay. In the student bars

JAY. No. No. Maybe I've, been struggling, with, my, everything, please, that's, understandable

DEAN. It isn't understandable at all, Jay. Because you certainly were in a position of power that time. Several positions. Truth be told, Claudia is not an ideal alibi. Would you really want her to come to your defence? An impressionable first year, she'd say you led her astray. Claudia's mother has a lot of influence, it's not the kind of thing I could leave off a reference. At the very least, you'd never work in university education again

JAY (*beat*). But given the choice… Between that, and being accused of, of. Fuck. Is this real? Have you, you can't have actually – Marjory Litherland? Just so you could? What have you done? What the fuck have you done?

DEAN. I imagine… I have given you a second chance

JAY. You crazy, fuck!

DEAN. And you don't have to thank me for it. Sorry, this is getting uncomfortable for me, you're floundering again. Take the opportunity, Jay! You choose who the public sees. A murderer of old maids? A philanderer of freshers? Or, are you the man who walked away, with some money in your pocket and your head held high? I'll give you thirty seconds to decide. And to help you… Because I never did get to see it… I have a certain piece of music –

JAY. No

DEAN. I know you're familiar with it, it will hone the mind –

JAY. Dean

DEAN. Never call me a fucking idiot again. (*Beat.*) And your time

JAY. Don't

DEAN. Starts

JAY. Please

DEAN. Now

> *The* Countdown *music plays.*
>
> *When the music finishes –*

06.

Years later.

JAY had aged, his clothes are torn.

DEAN remains untouched by time.

DEAN. Jay! I almost didn't recognise you. Been a long, long time. How did you get past security? Don't tell me. That call-out to the car park, the breach in the fence – that was a fake, wasn't it? A diversion. Mmm, perhaps you still have some allies on the inside then. I like the term now: 'allies'. It reminds me I still have enemies. Don't worry, we'll find them. I'll speak to the Guard Captain when he returns. Even so, getting back onto campus, Jay, let alone into the building, that's an impressive feat. Identity checkpoints, guards in towers… I bet you didn't even scan a student ID card at the front gate, that's a new rule. One of many. Well, here we are. I'd offer you a seat, but. We never did buy back those chairs. It's better this way. Classrooms, lectures, everybody stands to attention. Everybody salutes. Is there something I can help you with? Before you're arrested?

JAY. Can you hear yourself?

DEAN. Of course I can

JAY. This goes against… everything a university should be

DEAN. And what's that? Free? Liberal? Aside from the odd, skirmish, this university has been running rather well, thank you. Everything is streamlined. Secure. Between you and me… Sam Neill was a bit of a mistake. Power went to his head

JAY. I bet _he_ has a chair

DEAN. Not so much a chair as a throne. But we get by. He's not too invested in the administrative side of things

JAY. Just sits back and watches the destruction

DEAN. We're going to build it all back up. We simply had to tear it down first. I have the Principal's full backing. Just as long as nothing gets in the way of funding. Money. A necessary evil. What did you do with your severance pay, Jay? I worry you wasted it, you haven't been looking after yourself

JAY. I invested it

DEAN. Oh yes? In what?

JAY. Do you really want to know? We academics. We started talking among ourselves. This wasn't the only institution to turn its back on progress. We had to fight back. Against a system… against every fucking idiot we'd ever encountered. And then there was the breakthrough

DEAN. What breakthrough?

JAY. I can't believe you're not aware of the news

DEAN. What news?

JAY. A tremendous advancement in science. It took years to research, retrain, reorganise, we gave it everything we had. But now we have the most incredible, cloning technology

DEAN. And how exactly have you used this… technology?

JAY. Take a guess. Take a biiiiiig guess. Giant. Gigantic. Jurassic

DEAN (_beat_). This is a joke

JAY. My sense of humour went extinct a long time ago

DEAN. No, no, nope

JAY. 'Denying the truth doesn't stop it being true', who said that? I just made it up. We'll say it was David Attenborough. He scratched it on my dinosaur lunch box

DEAN. You can't expect me to believe you, after all this time –

JAY. This isn't a film. This isn't a fake. This is real life, Dean. And it actually happened. On an island…

DEAN. When security comes back –

JAY. One hundred and twenty miles west of Costa Rica…

DEAN. I am throwing you out –

JAY. And today I returned. That call to the car park. The guards will find an empty van. If they survive long enough. Cos that breach in the fence. It wasn't fake. Wasn't even human

DEAN. Jay

JAY. Test specimens. We lost three colleagues in development, another two in transportation. Sandra, God bless Sandra. But I brought them here. And now they are free. Loose upon the campus. They will rip this system to shreds

DEAN. What have you done?

JAY. This is what you made me do! You pushed me to this. Never in a million years – never in a hundred and forty-five million years – you hear that?

DEAN. Didn't hear anything

JAY. Your guards. Call your security, ask them what they see

DEAN. They don't see anything

JAY. Can you watch them on the cameras? Let yourself be squeamish. Maybe they'll fight them back with chairs

DEAN. There's nothing to fight!

JAY. They're getting closer

DEAN. No you can't

JAY. Tell me you're scared

DEAN. No

JAY. Tell me you're terrified

DEAN. There's nothing out there!

JAY. But they're coming

DEAN. I can't believe you

JAY. They're coming

DEAN. I can't believe you

JAY. The dinosaurs are nearly here

DEAN. I <u>won't</u> believe you!

JAY. That's more like it. Goodbye, Dean. From one idiot to another

*

A Jurassic cacophony as the system is ripped to shreds.

Chaos, chaos, chaos.

And the dinosaurs arrive.

End.

A Nick Hern Book

It Walks Around The House At Night & Jurassic: Two Plays first published in Great Britain as a paperback original in 2026 by Nick Hern Books Limited, The Glasshouse, 49a Goldhawk Road, London W12 8QP, in association with ThickSkin Theatre

It Walks Around The House At Night copyright © 2026 Tim Foley
Jurassic copyright © 2026 Tim Foley

Tim Foley has asserted his right to be identified as the author of these works

Cover image by Sean Longmore
Production photography by Tommy Ga-Ken Wan

Designed and typeset by Nick Hern Books, London
Printed in Great Britain by Mimeo Ltd, Huntingdon, Cambridgeshire PE29 6XX

A CIP catalogue record for this book is available from the British Library

ISBN 978 1 83904 545 5

CAUTION All rights whatsoever in these plays are strictly reserved. Requests to reproduce the texts in whole or in part should be addressed to the publisher. This book may not be used, in whole or in part, for the development or training of artificial intelligence technologies or systems.

Amateur Performing Rights Applications for performance, including readings and excerpts, by amateurs in the English language should be addressed to the Performing Rights Department, Nick Hern Books, The Glasshouse, 49a Goldhawk Road, London W12 8QP, *tel* +44 (0)20 8749 4953, *email* rights@nickhernbooks.co.uk, except as follows:

Australia: ORiGiN Theatrical, *email* enquiries@originmusic.com.au, *web* www.origintheatrical.com.au

New Zealand: Play Bureau, 20 Rua Street, Mangapapa, Gisborne, 4010, *tel* +64 21 258 3998, *email* info@playbureau.com

United States and Canada: The Agency (London) Ltd, see details below

Professional Performing Rights Applications for performance by professionals in any medium and in any language throughout the world should be addressed to The Agency (London) Ltd, 24 Pottery Lane, Holland Park, London W11 4LZ, *fax* +44 (0)20 7727 9037, *email* info@theagency.co.uk

No performance of any kind may be given unless a licence has been obtained. Applications should be made before rehearsals begin. Publication of these plays does not necessarily indicate their availability for performance.

www.nickhernbooks.co.uk/environmental-policy

Nick Hern Books' authorised representative in the EU is
Easy Access System Europe – Mustamäe tee 50, 10621 Tallinn, Estonia
email gpsr.requests@easproject.com

www.nickhernbooks.co.uk

@nickhernbooks